Middle and Upper Level ISEE®

Verbal, Reading, and Writing

Larchmont Academics

LarchmontAcademics.com

Table of Contents

Preparing for the Test

What to Expect on the ISEE®

The ISEE® has five sections. This book will focus on the Verbal Reasoning, Reading Comprehension, and Essay sections.

Section	Number of Questions	Time Allotted
Verbal Reasoning	40	20 minutes
Quantitative Reasoning	37	35 minutes
Reading Comprehension	36	35 minutes
Mathematics Achievement	47	40 minutes
Essay	1 prompt	30 minutes

The **Verbal Reasoning** section includes twenty synonym questions and twenty fill-in-the-blank questions

The **Reading Comprehension** section includes six passages with six questions each. You will answer questions to show your understanding.

There are six types of questions:
Main Idea
Supporting Ideas
Inference
Vocabulary
Organization/Logic
Tone/Style/Figurative Language

The **Essay** section is a free response section. Most often, you will just be given one prompt. Occasionally, you will have two to pick from. The essay is sent directly to the schools and is not scored.

(This book does not cover the **Quantitative Reasoning** and **Mathematics Achievement** sections.)

ISEE Scoring

 Scoring the ISEE

The ISEE scoring process has a few steps. It starts with your **raw score** which is based on the number of questions you answered correctly. This is then converted into a **scaled score** which is accompanied by a **percentile rank**. This percentile represents how you compare to other test takers. So, if you are in the 89th percentile, this does not mean you answered 89 percent of questions correctly. Instead, it means scored higher than 89 percent of test-takers. Your percentile score is then converted into a **stanine score** with a scale marked from 1 to 9 (9 being the highest.)

Percentile ——Stanine

1-3 —— 1
4-10——2
11-22——3
23-39——4
40-59——5
60-76——6
77-88——7
89-95——8
96-99——9

Verbal Reasoning

Studying Vocabulary

⬆ Learn Key Prefixes and Roots

Prefix

A prefix is a group of letters at the beginning of the word that alter the meaning of the word. For example, un- is the prefix of "unhappy."

Study the following prefixes:

Ben-	Good	Beneficial, benevolent
Mal-	Bad	Malice, malign
Mis-	Bad	Misanthrope, mischance
Un-	Not	Unwelcome, unsatisfactory
Non-	Not	Nonessential, nonexistent
Anti-	Against	Antisocial, antipathy
Di/dif/dis-	Not, apart	Differ, disparity
Trans-	Across	Transfer, transpose
Pro-	Forward, before	Prologue, prominent
Magna/mag-	Great	Magnificent, magnitude
Sub-	Under, less	Submarine, subdued
Con-	With, together	Concur, consensus

Root

A root is the part of the word that contains the central meaning. For example, happy is the root word in "unhappy."

Study the following root words:

Act	do	Action, activate
Ami	love	Amicable, amiable
Anthro	human	Anthropology, misanthrope
Aud	hear	Audio, audible
Bio	life	Biology, biography
Chron	time	Chronological, synchronize
Dict	speak	Diction, dictate
Graph	write or draw	Autograph, biography
morph	form	Amorphous, metamorphous
Phon	sound	Telephone, phonics
Port	carry	Transport, export
Tact	touch	Tactile, contact
Viv	Alive	Vivacious, vivid

Picture the Word

When studying words you don't know, imagine a picture in your head to help you remember it. You can even use sounds in the word to help you remember.

Examples:

Pugnacious: Eager to fight
Picture a pug fighting.

Gregarious: Talkative
Picture a kid named Greg who won't stop talking.

 # Study by Category

Study groups of words with the same meaning. By studying many words with the same definition, you are just memorizing words rather than many different definitions. NOTE: This may not help you be able to use the words well, but it will help you know them well enough to do well on a standardized test.

You can use the word list below as a starting point. After each practice section, you should also add any words you don't know to the relevant list or start a new list.

Vocabulary List by Category

Friendly

Collegial	Friendly
Amiable	Friendly
Genial	Friendly
Benevolent	Friendly
Compassionate	Friendly (showing sympathy)
Empathy	Friendly (showing sympathy)
Amicable	Friendly
Affable	Friendly
Cordial	Friendly
Compatible	Friendly (suited)

Praise

Flatter	Praise
Acclaim	Praise
Commend	Praise
Laud	Praise
Extol	Praise

Loyalty

Fidelity	Loyalty
Allegiance	Loyalty
Devotion	Loyalty
Homage	Loyalty

Stubborn

Steadfast	Stubborn
Headstrong	Stubborn
Obstinate	Stubborn
Resolute	Stubborn
Dogmatic	Stubborn
Obdurate	Stubborn
Intransigent	Stubborn

Hardworking

Diligent	Hardworking
Industrial	Hardworking
Persistent	Hardworking
Laborious	Hardworking

Annoy

Exasperate	Annoy
Vex	Annoy
Agitate	Annoy

Angry/Fight

Pugnacious	Angry
Indignant	Angry
Belligerent	Angry (fight)
Irate	Angry
Livid	Angry
Cantankerous	Angry

Unconcerned

Aloof	Unconcerned
Nonchalant	Unconcerned
Apathetic	Unconcerned
Indifferent	Unconcerned
Oblivious	Unaware
Ignorant	Unaware

Changing/Not Reliable

Fickle	Changing/Not Reliable
Temperamental	Changing/Not Reliable
Volatile	Changing/Not Reliable
Flighty	Changing/Not Reliable
Arbitrary	Changing/Not Reliable (random)
Spontaneous	Changing/Not Reliable (random)
Mutable	Changing/Not Reliable
Erratic	Changing/Not Reliable

Hate

Malicious	Hate
Disdain	Hateful
Abhor	Hate
Animosity	Hate
Hostility	Hate
Loathing	Hate
Detest	Hate
Acrimony	Hate
Enmity	Hate
Scorn	Hate
Rancor	Hate

Put Down

Belittle	Put Down
Jeer	Put Down (laugh at)
Snub	Put Down (ignore)
Condescend	Put Down
Denigrate	Put Down
Denounce	Put Down
Decry	Put Down
Deride	Put Down
Vilify	Put Down

Lively

Vivacious	Lively
Exuberant	Lively
Extroverted	Lively
Charismatic	Lively (charming)
Ebullient	Lively

Reserved

Introverted	Reserved
Diffident	Reserved
Timid	Reserved
Meek	Reserved
Docile	Reserved
Subdued	Reserved
Reticent	Reserved
Demure	Reserved

Scold

Admonish	Scold
Reprimand	Scold
Berate	Scold
Rebuke	Scold

Weak

Feeble	Weak
Frail	Weak
Vulnerable	Weak

Difficult/Difficulty

Adversity	Difficulty
Plight	Difficulty
Predicament	Difficulty
Strenuous	Difficult
Toil	Difficult

Trick

Deceive	Trick
Swindle	Trick
Hoax	Trick
Defraud	Trick
Treachery	Trick (cheat)
Cunning	Tricky

Sad

Dismal	Sad
Bleak	Sad
Remorse	Sad (regret)
Dejected	Sad
Melancholy	Sad
Lament	Sad
Dour	Sad
Despondent	Sad
Morose	Sad

Plentiful

Copious	Plentiful
Prolific	Plentiful
Ample	Plentiful
Abundant	Plentiful
Bountiful	Plentiful
Profuse	Plentiful

Brief

Concise	Brief
Succinct	Brief
Terse	Brief
Abridged	Brief
Truncated	Brief

Clever

Shrewd	Clever
Astute	Clever
Ingenious	Clever
Perceptive	Clever
Judicious	Clever
Prudent	Clever (sensible/careful)
Discerning	Clever
Incisive	Clever

Snobby

Bombastic	Snobby
Elitist	Snobby
Haughty	Snobby
Patronize	Snobby
Pompous	Snobby
Pretentious	Snobby

Make Feel Better

Alleviate	Make feel better
Appease	Make feel better
Mollify	Make feel better
Temper	Make feel better
Mitigate	Make feel better

Joy

Elated	Joy
Euphoria	Joy
Felicity	Joy
Buoyant	Joy
Mirth	Joy

Agreement

Accord	Agreement
Concord	Agreement
Concur	Agreement
Consensus	Agreement

Ordinary

Banal	Ordinary
Trite	Ordinary
Hackneyed	Ordinary
Insipid	Ordinary
Mundane	Ordinary

Other (After taking the practice tests, add more words to study here.)

Dwell	Live
Barren	Empty

_____   _____

_____   _____

_____   _____

_____   _____

_____   _____

_____   _____

_____   _____

_____   _____

_____   _____

Approaching the Questions

🎯 Cover, Guess, Check

The wrong answers can often be tricky. Sometimes, they are even trying to trick you! To avoid getting sidetracked by the wrong answers, cover the answer choices, guess the word, and then check the answer choices,

Cover

Cover up the answers and focus just on the question.

Guess

For synonyms, guess the answer by saying what the word means in your head.

For fill-ins, guess a word that fits in the blank.

Check

Look at the answer choices and find a similar word.

I Don't Know that Word!

Studying vocabulary is very important for this section, but if you don't know a word on the test, you may still be able to figure out the answer.

1. Eliminate two answer choices that are synonyms.
    If two words mean the same, exact thing, neither of them can be the correct answer! Eliminate both of them!

2. Look for prefixes and roots that you know.
    Study the prefixes and roots beginning on page 8 for clues to help figure out the word.

3. Decide if the word seems positive or negative and choose your answer based on that. You often will have more of an intuition for this than you think!

4. For fill-ins, only choose the word you don't know once you have eliminated all of the words you do know.

Rephrase the Fill-In Questions

If you are having trouble understanding a fill-in-the-blank question, try putting it into your own words. You can also most often ignore proper nouns. Do your best to simplify it. You could even turn it into a question in your mind.

Find the Definition in the Sentence

There will always be a part of the sentence that gives a synonym or antonym for the word in the blank. Find and underline that part of the sentence. Use this to determine the definition of the word for which you are looking.

✏️ Try it!
Practice the Cover, Guess, Check Method:

1. ABRUPT

    Without looking at the answer choices, write a synonym here: _____

    Now, find an answer that matches:

    (A) Indifferent

    (B) Orderly

    (C) Unexpected

    (D) Tired

2. FRAIL

    Without looking at the answer choices, write a synonym here: _____

    Now, find an answer that matches:

    (A) Clear

    (B) Quick

    (C) Thoughtful

    (D) Weak

3. INSUBORDINATE

    Without looking at the answer choices, write a synonym here: _____

    Now, find an answer that matches:

    (A) Rebellious

    (B) Disputed

    (C) Compliant

    (D) Doubtful

4. PERCEPTION

    <u>Without looking at the answer choices, write a synonym here:</u> _____

    Now, find an answer that matches:

    (A) Disagreement
    (B) Eagerness
    (C) Fatigue
    (D) Insight

5. TRANQUIL

    <u>Without looking at the answer choices, write a synonym here:</u> _____

    Now, find an answer that matches:

    (A) Calm
    (B) Praise
    (C) Excuse
    (D) Commend

Practice Looking for Roots and Prefixes:

6. BENEVOLENT

    (A) Kind

    (B) Lively

    (C) Rich

    (D) Bossy

7. EMPATHY

    (A) Compassion

    (B) Stubbornness

    (C) Strength

    (D) Energy

8. MALICIOUS

    (A) Warm

    (B) Extreme

    (C) Hateful

    (D) Logical

9. DICTUM

    (A) Friendship

    (B) Statement

    (C) Theft

    (D) Distance

10. AMORPHOUS

    (A) Thoughtful

    (B) Shy

    (C) Shapeless

    (D) Large

Practice the Cover, Guess, Check Method with Sentence Completion:

11. While climbing Mt. Kilimanjaro is strenuous, the advanced hikers who have reached the peak _____ its beautiful views.

Without looking at the answer choices, write a guess for the blank here:

_____

Now, find an answer that matches:

(A) Laud
(B) Disengage
(C) Denounce
(D) Enhance

12. The week-long wildfire destroyed everything in its path, leaving the land in the hills almost completely _____.

Without looking at the answer choices, write a guess for the blank here:

_____

Now, find an answer that matches:

(A) Fertile
(B) Desolate
(C) Productive
(D) Soaked

13. The historians wanted to give up after searching through countless files for the record they sought out, but the drive of the leader led them to _____.

Without looking at the answer choices, write a guess for the blank here:

_____

Now, find an answer that matches:

(A) Persist

(B) Surrender

(C) Encourage

(D) Depart

14. The skeptical musicians _____ the jazz artist's improvisational style; however, they quickly took back their words when the artist rose to fame.

<u>Without looking at the answer choices, write a guess for the blank here:</u>

_____

Now, find an answer that matches:

(A) Praised

(B) Criticized

(C) Soothed

(D) Emulated

15. Because Kaila's employer was not able to support her, she was forced to _____ her source of income when she became too sick to go to work.

<u>Without looking at the answer choices, write a guess for the blank here:</u>

_____

Now, find an answer that matches:

(A) Forgo

(B) Supplement

(C) Examine

(D) Trust

Practice Additional Sentence Completion Strategies:

16. When the Metropolitan Museum of Art acquired the _____ work of Edgar Degas, hundreds of people from all over the world rushed to the museum to see the famous masterpiece from 1880.

    <u>Cross out what you can while keeping the sentence functional:</u>

    When the Metropolitan Museum of Art acquired the _____ work of Edgar Degas, hundreds of people from all over the world rushed to the museum to see the famous masterpiece from 1880.

    Example:

    When the ~~Metropolitan~~ Museum ~~of Art~~ acquired the _____ work ~~of Edgar Degas~~, hundreds of people ~~from all over the world~~ rushed to the museum ~~to see the famous masterpiece from 1880.~~

    <u>Guess:</u> _____

    (A) Disappointing
    (B) Controversial
    (C) Vigorous
    (D) Prominent

17. Although Stefan acted _____ about the upcoming presidential election when he was with his friends at school, he was actually very passionate about one of the candidates and was planning to go door to door helping with the campaign.

Cross out what you can while keeping the sentence functional:

Although Stefan acted _____ about the upcoming presidential election when he was with his friends at school, he was actually very passionate about one of the candidates and was planning to go door to door helping with the campaign.

Guess: _____

    (A) Indifferent

    (B) Concerned

    (C) Enthusiastic

    (D) Weak

18. Harry Clifford's novel, *The Advent of the Storm*, is not known for its _____ language, instead, the author uses many descriptive adjectives and details about the scenery making it a very lengthy read.

Underline the part of the sentence that defines the blank.

Guess: _____

    (A) Concise

    (B) Sophisticated

    (C) Verbose

    (D) Elevated

19. When the howling of the coyotes _____, people who hear it assume that there must be a full moon because coyotes are known to increase their hunting activities under the light of the moon.

Underline the part of the sentence that defines the blank.

Guess: _____

    (A) Subsides

    (B) Intensifies

    (C) Randomizes

    (D) Migrates

20. The technology company's employee had hoped the executives would support her proposal for the new device, but they immediately _____ it without explanation.
Underline the OPPOSITE of the word in the blank.

Guess: _____

    (A) Dismissed

    (B) Entrusted

    (C) Developed

    (D) Defended

Answers and Explanations:

1. ABRUPT
    Guess Example: Sudden
    Answer: (C) Unexpected

2. FRAIL
    Guess Example: feeble
    Answer: (D) Unexpected

3. INSUBORDINATE
    Guess Example: not compliant
    Answer: (A) Rebellious

4. PERCEPTION
    Guess Example: sense
    Answer: (D) Insight

5. TRANQUIL
    Guess example: peaceful
    Answer: (A) Calm

6. BENEVOLENT
    Prefix: Bene (good)
    Answer: (A) Kind

7. EMPATHY
    Root: Path (feel)
    Answer: (A) Compassionate

8. MALICIOUS
    Prefix: Mal (bad)
    Answer: (C) Hateful

9. DICTUM
    Root: Dict (speak)
    Answer: (B) Statement

10. AMORPHOUS
    <u>Prefix</u>: a- (not) Root: morph (shape)
    Answer: (C) Shapeless

11. While climbing Mt. Kilimanjaro is strenuous, the advanced hikers who have reached the peak _____ its beautiful views.

    <u>Guess Example</u>: Praise
    Answer: (A) Laud
    (Note: If you don't know this word, think of applaud and you won't forget!)

12. The week-long wildfire destroyed everything in its path, leaving the land in the hills almost completely _____.

    <u>Guess Example</u>: Barren
    Answer: (B) Desolate

13. The historians wanted to give up after searching through countless files for the record they sought out, but the drive leader led them to _____.

    <u>Guess Example</u>: Keep going
    Answer: (A) Persist

14. The skeptical musicians _____ the jazz artist's improvisational style; however, they quickly took back their words when the artist rose to fame.

    <u>Guess Example</u>: Didn't like
    Answer: (B) Criticized

15. Because Kaila's employer was not able to support her, she was forced to _____ her source of income when she became too sick to go to work.

    <u>Guess Example</u>: Give up
    Answer: (A) Forgo

16. When the Metropolitan Museum of Art acquired the _____ work of Edgar Degas, hundreds of people from all over the world rushed to the museum to see the famous masterpiece from 1880.

Simplified: When the museum-acquired the _____ work hundreds of people rushed to the museum.
Guess Example: Famous
Answer: (D) Prominent

17. Although Stefan acted _____ about the upcoming presidential election when he was with his friends at school, he was actually very passionate about one of the candidates and was planning to go door to door helping with the campaign.

Simplified: Although he acted _____ about the upcoming election, he was actually very passionate.
Example Guess: Like he didn't care
Answer: (A) Indifferent

18. Harry Clifford's novel, *The Advent of the Storm*, is not known for its _____ language, instead, the author uses many descriptive adjectives and details about the scenery making it a very lengthy read.

Definition: *Opposite of* "many descriptive adjectives and details"
Guess: Brief
Answer: (A) Concise

19. When the howling of the coyotes _____, people who hear it assume that there must be a full moon because coyotes are known to increase their hunting activities under the light of the moon.

Definition: "increase"
Guess: Increases
Answer: (B) Intensifies

20. The technology company's employee had hoped the executives would support her proposal for the new device, but they immediately _____ it without explanation.

Definition: *Opposite of* "support"
Guess: Cut
Answer: (A) Dismissed

Reading Comprehension

Timing Strategies

Keep Track of Your Timing

36 Questions – 35 Minutes

Your goal is to spend just under six minutes on each passage. Check your time after you finish each passage to make sure you are on track. Some passages will be easier than others. Going quickly through the easy passages, will allow you to spend more time on the harder passages.

It is recommended that you spend 1-2 minutes previewing each reading passage. You should then spend the majority of your time finding the answer to each question.

Preview the passage

You should only spend 1-2 minutes reading the passage before looking at the questions. Think of this as a preview. Your goal is to get the main idea. Use the rest of the six minutes to find the answer to each question in the passage.

Previewing the Passage

The Goal

When you initially read the passage, the goal is just to get an idea of the overall topic and structure. Your goal is not to remember all the details. You will only be asked six questions, and you will want to go back to the passage to find the answers. So, spend the first one to two minutes previewing the passage. The 2 – 1 – 2 strategy is one proven way to do this.

The 2 – 1 – 2 Strategy

When you first read the passage, ONLY read the first **2** sentences of the passage, the first **1** sentence of each paragraph, and the last **2** sentences of the passage.

This will help you get the main idea of the passage without letting the details get you sidetracked. The first time you do it, you may feel confused, but keep practicing and you will see why it works!

✏ Try it!

Highlight the first **2** sentences of the passage, the first **1** sentence of each paragraph, and the last **2** sentences of the passage.

Passage 1:

1 In newspaper literature, women made
2 their entrance at an early period and in an
3 important manner. The first *daily* newspaper
4 in the world was established and edited by a
5 woman, Elizabeth Mallet, in London, in
6 March 1702. It was called *The Daily Courant*.
7 In her salutatory, Mrs. Mallet declared she
8 had established her paper to "spare the public
9 at least half the impertinences which the
10 ordinary papers contain." Thus, the first daily
11 paper was made reformatory in character by
12 its wise, woman founder.
13   The first newspaper printed in Rhode
14 Island was by Anna Franklin in 1732. She
15 was a printer to the colony, supplied blanks to
16 the public officers, published pamphlets, etc.
17 In 1745 she printed for the colonial
18 government an edition of the laws comprising
19 three hundred and forty pages.
20   Sarah Josepha Hale established a ladies'
21 magazine in Boston in 1827. She afterward
22 moved to Philadelphia, by associating with
23 Louis Godey, and assuming the editorship
24 of *Godey's Lady's Book*. This magazine was
25 followed by many others, of which Mrs.
26 Kirkland, Mrs. Osgood, Mrs. Ellet, Mrs.
27 Sigourney, and women of like character were
28 editors or contributors. These early magazines
29 published many steel and colored engravings,
30 not only of fashion, but also reproductions of

31 works of art, giving the first important
32 impulse to the art of engraving in this country.
33   Many other periodicals and papers by
34 women now appeared throughout the country.
35 Mrs. Anne Royal edited, for a quarter of a
36 century, a paper called *The Huntress*. In 1827
37 Lydia Maria Child published a paper for
38 children called *The Juvenile Miscellany*, and
39 in 1841 she assumed the editorship of *The
40 Anti-Slavery Standard*, in New York, which
41 she ably conducted for eight years. *The Dial*,
42 in Boston, a transcendental quarterly, edited
43 by Margaret Fuller, made its appearance in
44 1840; its contributors, among whom were
45 Ralph Waldo Emerson, Bronson Alcott,
46 Theodore Parker, William H. Channing, and
47 the nature-loving Thoreau, were some of the
48 most profound thinkers of the time.
49   *The Lily*, a temperance monthly, was
50 started in Seneca Falls, N. Y., in 1849, by
51 Amelia Bloomer, the editor and publisher. It
52 also advocated women's rights and attained
53 circulation in nearly every state and territory
54 of the Union.
55   In the United States the list of women's
56 fashion papers, with their women editors and
57 correspondents, is numerous. If the proverb
58 that "the pen is mightier than the sword" is
59 true, a woman's skill and force in using this
60 mightier weapon will soon change the destiny
61 of the world.

Check it!

Make sure your highlighting looks like it does below! When using the 2-1-2 strategy, this is all you should read when you first preview the passage. Remember, you can go back to find the details later!

Passage 1:

1   In newspaper literature, women made
2   their entrance at an early period and in an
3   important manner. The first *daily* newspaper
4   in the world was established and edited by a
5   woman, Elizabeth Mallet, in London, in
6   March 1702. It was called *The Daily Courant*.
7   In her salutatory, Mrs. Mallet declared she
8   had established her paper to "spare the public
9   at least half the impertinences which the
10 ordinary papers contain." Thus, the first daily
11 paper was made reformatory in character by
12 its wise, woman founder.
13   The first newspaper printed in Rhode
14 Island was by Anna Franklin in 1732. She
15 was a printer to the colony, supplied blanks to
16 the public officers, published pamphlets, etc.
17 In 1745 she printed for the colonial
18 government an edition of the laws comprising
19 three hundred and forty pages.
20   Sarah Josepha Hale established a ladies'
21 magazine in Boston in 1827. She afterward
22 moved to Philadelphia, by associating with
23 Louis Godey, and assuming the editorship
24 of *Godey's Lady's Book*. This magazine was
25 followed by many others, of which Mrs.
26 Kirkland, Mrs. Osgood, Mrs. Ellet, Mrs.
27 Sigourney, and women of like character were
28 editors or contributors. These early magazines
29 published many steel and colored engravings,
30 not only of fashion, but also reproductions of

31 works of art, giving the first important
32 impulse to the art of engraving in this country.
33   Many other periodicals and papers by
34 women now appeared throughout the country.
35 Mrs. Anne Royal edited, for a quarter of a
36 century, a paper called *The Huntress*. In 1827
37 Lydia Maria Child published a paper for
38 children called *The Juvenile Miscellany*, and
39 in 1841 she assumed the editorship of *The
40 Anti-Slavery Standard*, in New York, which
41 she ably conducted for eight years. *The Dial*,
42 in Boston, a transcendental quarterly, edited
43 by Margaret Fuller, made its appearance in
44 1840; its contributors, among whom were
45 Ralph Waldo Emerson, Bronson Alcott,
46 Theodore Parker, William H. Channing, and
47 the nature-loving Thoreau, were some of the
48 most profound thinkers of the time.
49   *The Lily*, a temperance monthly, was
50 started in Seneca Falls, N. Y., in 1849, by
51 Amelia Bloomer, the editor and publisher. It
52 also advocated women's rights and attained
53 circulation in nearly every state and territory
54 of the Union.
55   In the United States the list of women's
56 fashion papers, with their women editors and
57 correspondents, is numerous. If the proverb
58 that "the pen is mightier than the sword" is
59 true, a woman's skill and force in using this
60 mightier weapon must soon change the
61 destiny of the world.

The Skim Strategy

If the passage is short or the 2 – 1 – 2 strategy isn't your style, try skimming the passage. For each paragraph, fully read the first sentence and then quickly read the rest looking for the main idea. Skip over details like names, dates, and places.

Remember, the goal is to get the main idea of the passage and to have an idea of what is discussed in each paragraph.

 **Try it!**

For practice, set a timer for 40 seconds. Skim this passage.

1   It is by attention that we gather and mass
2 our mental energy upon the critical and
3 important points in our thinking. *The*
4 *concentration of the mind's energy on one*
5 *object of thought is attention.*
6   Everyone knows what it is to attend. A
7 story so fascinating that we cannot leave it,
8 the critical points in a game, an interesting
9 sermon or lecture, a sparkling conversation—
10 all of these compel our attention. So
11 completely is our mind's energy centered on
12 them and withdrawn from other things that we
13 are scarcely aware of what is going on about
14 us.
15   We are also familiar with another kind of
16 attention. For we all have read a dull story,
17 watched a slow game, listened to a lecture or
18 sermon that drags, and taken part in a
19 conversation that was a bore. We gave these
20 things our attention, but only with effort. Our
21 mind's energy seemed to center on anything
22 rather than the matter at hand. A thousand
23

24 objects from outside enticed us away, and it
25 required the frequent "mental jerk" to bring us
26 to the subject at hand. And when brought
27 back to our thought problem we felt the
28 constant "tug" of mind to be free again.
29   But this very effort of the mind to free
30 itself from one object of thought that it may
31 busy itself with another is *because attention is*
32 *solicited by this other*. Some object in our
33 field of consciousness is always exerting an
34 appeal for attention, and to attend *to* one thing
35 is always to attend *away from* a multitude of
36 other things upon which the thought might
37 rest. We may therefore say that attention is
38 constantly *selecting,* in our stream of thought,
39 those aspects that are to receive emphasis and
40 consideration. From moment to moment, it
41 determines the points at which our mental
42 energy shall be centered.

Now, respond to these questions:

What is the main idea of the
passage?

What are some of the topics
covered?

☑ Check it!

What is the main idea of the passage?

The passage is about attention.

What are some of the topics covered?
- *Definition of attention*
- *Paying attention to interesting things*
- *Taking attention away from some things and giving it to other things*

THAT IS ALL YOU NEED TO KNOW! The goal of the preview is to get the main idea. Once you get to the questions, you can then go back for the details.

Approaching the Questions

 Restate the question

If you don't know what the question is asking, you can't answer it! For more complicated questions, rephrase them in your own words. If the question doesn't end with a question mark, phrase it in a way that does.

Example:

It can be implied from the passage that the "our," referred to in lines 25 and 33, refers to whom...

<u>Rephrase it!</u>

Who does the "our" refer to?

 Reading Comprehension Is a Scavenger Hunt!

Because the ISEE is a standardized test, all the answers have to be provable. That means that the answers are in the passage, and it is your job to find them!

If you spend less time on your initial reading, you will have more time to go into the passage and find your answers. They are all there, you just need to find them! As we go through each question type, we will give you some hints to help you know where to look.

 Cover, Guess, Check

The wrong answers can often be tricky. Sometimes, they are even trying to trick you! To avoid getting sidetracked by the wrong answers, cover the answer choices, find your answer, and then check the answer choices,

Cover

Cover up the answers and focus just on the question.

Guess

Go into the passage and find the answer. Guess what you think the answer will be.

Check

Look for your answer or something close to your answer in the answer choices

Main Idea Questions

What are main idea questions asking?

Main idea questions ask you to identify the central point of the passage. The first question for a passage is often a main idea question.

Here are some examples:

1. Which sentence best expresses the main idea of the passage?
2. Which best states the main point of the paragraph (lines ----)?
3. What is the primary purpose of the passage?

Where should I look?

If the question is about the passage as a whole, look at the first two sentences and last two sentences of the passage.

If the question is about one paragraph, look at the first sentence and the last sentence of the paragraph.

Sometimes, the other answer choices will be true (an accurate reflection of some details in the passage), but not every detail is the main idea. Looking at the beginning and the end will help you find the main idea.

Try it!

Now, try it with these questions. For this practice, you do NOT need to read the passage first. Simply use the passage to find your answer.

1. What is the main idea of paragraph 3 (lines 20 – 30)?
    A. Active volcanoes are very dangerous
    B. There is a possibility that an extinct volcano could erupt
    C. Extinct volcanoes form crater lakes
    D. Extinct volcanoes no longer have the potential to erupt

Use this passage: (Remember, don't read the whole thing, just read the first and last lines of paragraph 3)

1   A volcano that throws out molten rock, vapor,
2   and gases is known as an *active volcano*. An active
3   volcano, however, is only correctly said to be in a
4   state of eruption when the quantity of the molten
5   rock, lava, or vapor it throws out greatly exceeds
6   the ordinary amount.
7   Sometimes the volcanic activity so greatly
8   decreases that the molten rock or lava no longer
9   rises in the crater, but, on the contrary, begins to
10 sink. The lava then begins to harden on the surface,
11 and, if the time is sufficient, the hardened part
12 extends for a considerable distance downward. In
13 this way the opening connecting the crater with the
14 molten lava below becomes gradually closed, the
15 volcano being thus shut up, or corked, just as a
16 bottle is tightly closed using a cork driven into the
17 opening at its top to prevent the escape of the liquid
18 it contains. A volcano thus choked or corked up is
19 said to be *extinct*.
20 When we speak of an extinct volcano, we do not
21 mean that the volcano will never again become
22 active. A volcano does not cease to erupt because
23 there are no more molten materials in the earth to
24 escape, but simply because its cork or crust of
25 hardened lava has been driven in so tightly that the
26 chances of its ever being loosened again seem to be
27 very small. But small as the chances may seem we

28 must not forget that the volcano may at any time
29 become active or go into its old business of
30 throwing out materials through its crater.
31 Since the plug of hardened lava in the volcanic
32 crater is generally at a much lower level than the
33 top of the crater, the crater will soon become filled
34 to a greater or less depth with water, produced
35 either by the rain or by the melting of the snow that
36 falls on the top of the mountain. Crater lakes, often
37 of very great depths, are common in extinct
38 volcanoes.
39 Of course, when an extinct volcano again
40 becomes active, two things must happen if the
41 eruption is explosive. In the first place, the force of
42 the explosion must be sufficiently great to loosen
43 the stopper or plug of hardened lava which stops it.
44 But besides the breaking up of the stopper, the lake
45 in the crater of the volcano is thrown out along with
46 the cinders or ashes, producing very destructive
47 flows of what are called aqueous lava or mud
48 streams. These streams flow down the sides of the
49 mountain, carrying with them immense quantities
50 of both the ashes thrown out during the eruption, or
51 those that have collected around the sides of the
52 crater during previous eruptions. Very frequently,
53 these streams of aqueous lava produce greater
54 destruction than the molten lava.

---

2. What is the main idea of this passage?
    A. It can be very difficult to pay attention to boring stories
    B. Attention is how we concentrate our mental energy
    C. Attending an event is very similar to attending something with your mind
    D. Inattentiveness requires mental effort

Use this passage:

1   It is by attention that we gather and mass
2   our mental energy upon the critical and
3   important points in our thinking. *The*
4   *concentration of the mind's energy on one*
5   *object of thought is attention.*
6   Everyone knows what it is to attend. A
7   story so fascinating that we cannot leave it,
8   the critical points in a game, an interesting
9   sermon or lecture, a sparkling conversation—
10 all of these compel our attention. So
11 completely is our mind's energy centered on
12 them and withdrawn from other things that we
13 are scarcely aware of what is going on about
14 us.
15   We are also familiar with another kind of
16 attention. We all have read a dull story,
17 watched a slow game, listened to a lecture or
18 sermon that drags, and taken part in a
19 conversation that was a bore. We gave these
20 things our attention, but only with effort. Our
21 mind's energy seemed to center on anything

22 rather than the matter at hand. A thousand
23 objects from outside enticed us away, and it
24 required the frequent "mental jerk" to bring us
25 to the subject at hand. And when brought
26 back to our thought problem we felt the
27 constant "tug" of mind to be free again.
28   But this very effort of the mind to free
29 itself from one object of thought that it may
30 busy itself with another is *because attention is*
31 *solicited by this other.* Some object in our
32 field of consciousness is always exerting an
33 appeal for attention, and to attend *to* one thing
34 is always to attend *away from* a multitude of
35 other things upon which the thought might
36 rest. We may therefore say that attention is
37 constantly *selecting,* in our stream of thought,
38 those aspects that are to receive emphasis and
39 consideration. From moment to moment, it
40 determines the points at which our mental
41 energy shall be centered.

50

Explanation:

The correct answer is B. - Attention is how we concentrate our mental energy.

<u>First two lines</u>: "It is by attention that we gather and mass our mental energy upon the critical and important points in our thinking. The concentration of the mind's energy on one object of thought is attention."

<u>Last two lines</u>: "We may therefore say that attention is constantly selecting, in our stream of thought, those aspects that are to receive emphasis and consideration. From moment to moment, it determines the points at which our mental energy shall be centered."

Both sections discuss how we center our mental energy. The phrase mental energy is even used multiple times in these sentences.

---

3. What is the main idea of the first paragraph of this passage (lines 1 – 11)?
   A. The first newspaper established by a woman was created to bring about reform
   B. Women wrote about very popular topics in newspapers
   C. Female writers fought for women's rights in politics
   D. Men significantly censored women's writing

1   In newspaper literature, women made their
2 entrance at an early period and in an important
3 manner. The first *daily* newspaper in the world
4 was established and edited by a woman, Elizabeth
5 Mallet, in London, in March 1702. It was
6 called *The Daily Courant*. In her salutatory, Mrs.
7 Mallet declared she had established her paper to
8 "spare the public at least half the impertinences
9 which the ordinary papers contain." Thus, the first
10 daily paper was made reformatory in character by
11 its wise woman founder.
12   The first newspaper printed in Rhode Island
13 was by Anna Franklin in 1732. She was a printer
14 to the colony, supplied blanks to the public
15 officers, published pamphlets, etc. In 1745 she
16 printed for the colonial government an edition of
17 the laws comprising three hundred and forty
18 pages.
19   Sarah Josepha Hale established a ladies'
20 magazine in Boston in 1827. She afterward moved
21 to Philadelphia, by associating with Louis Godey,
22 and assuming the editorship of *Godey's Lady's*
23 *Book*. This magazine was followed by many
24 others, of which Mrs. Kirkland, Mrs. Osgood,
25 Mrs. Ellet, Mrs. Sigourney, and women of like
26 character were editors or contributors. These early
27 magazines published many steel and colored
28 engravings, not only of fashion but also
29 reproductions of works of art, giving the first

30 important impulse to the art of engraving in this
31 country.
32   Many other periodicals and papers by women
33 now appeared throughout the country. Mrs. Anne
34 Royal edited, for a quarter of a century, a paper
35 called *The Huntress*. In 1827 Lydia Maria Child
36 published a paper for children called *The Juvenile*
37 *Miscellany*, and in 1841 she assumed the
38 editorship of *The Anti-Slavery Standard*, in New
39 York, which she ably conducted for eight
40 years. *The Dial*, in Boston, a transcendental
41 quarterly, edited by Margaret Fuller, made its
42 appearance in 1840; its contributors, among
43 whom were Ralph Waldo Emerson, Bronson
44 Alcott, Theodore Parker, William H. Channing,
45 and the nature-loving Thoreau, were some of the
46 most profound thinkers of the time.
47   *The Lily*, a temperance monthly, was started
48 in Seneca Falls, N. Y., in 1849, by Amelia
49 Bloomer, the editor and publisher. It also
50 advocated women's and rights and attained
51 circulation in nearly every state and territory of
52 the Union.
53   In the United States the list of women's
54 fashion papers, with their women editors and
55 correspondents, is numerous. If the proverb that
56 "the pen is mightier than the sword" is true, a
57 woman's skill and force in using this mightier
58 weapon must soon change the destinies of the
59 world.

Explanation:
The correct answer is A. - The first newspaper established by a woman was created to bring about reform.

<u>First line</u>: "In newspaper literature women made their entrance at an early period and in an important manner."
<u>Last line</u>: "Thus, the first daily paper was made reformatory in character by its wise woman founder."

The last sentence directly states the answer. It says that the first paper was for reform.

---

4. Which statement best describes the main idea of this passage?
   A. Ostriches use their wings when they turn
   B. Ostriches are giant creatures which makes them largely unable to move
   C. Ostriches are vicious and must only be observed from afar
   D. Ostriches cannot fly, but their movement is still interesting to observe

1   The ostrich is the giant amongst living
2 birds, the full-grown male standing some 8 feet
3 high, and weighing about 300 lbs. It is
4 flightless, the wings being smaller, in
5 proportion to the size of the body. But the
6 energy that other birds employ in sustaining
7 flight, in the ostrich is instead expended in
8 running, so that it has reached a high degree of
9 speed—no less, in fact, than twenty-six miles
10 an hour.
11   When at full speed, it is generally
12 believed the ostrich derives no small help from
13 the wings, which are used sail-wise. Nor is this
14 belief by any means a modern one, for all of us
15 must be familiar with Job's observations on
16 this subject: "What time she lifteth up her
17 wings on high, she scorneth the horse and his
18 rider." The wings are never used in running at
19 full speed, but are of much service in turning,
20 "enabling the bird to double abruptly, even
21 when going at top speed." In justice to the older
22 observers, however, it must be remarked that
23 ostriches do run with raised wings, but only at
24 the commencement of the run, or in covering a

25 short distance, when the pace may be
26 considerable; but if circumstances demand
27 "full speed ahead," they are held close to the
28 body, where they offer the least resistance to
29 speed.
30   With the gradual perfection of its
31 running powers, there has followed a gradual
32 change in the form of the leg. This change has
33 taken place by a reduction in the number of
34 toes. Of the original five with which its
35 ancestors began life only two now remain—the
36 third and fourth. The third is of great size,
37 having waxed great at the expense of the other
38 toes, a growth which seems to be still in
39 progress, since the fourth toe is undoubtedly
40 dwindling. It is very small and gives
41 unmistakable signs of growing smaller since it
42 has now become nailless. When it has quite
43 disappeared, the ostrich, like the horse, will
44 have but a single toe on each foot—the third.
45 The dainty, mincing step of the ostrich is a
46 delight to watch, and, thanks to the Zoological
47 Gardens, this can be done even in smoky
48 London.

Explanation:

The correct answer is D - Ostriches cannot fly, but their movement is still interesting to observe.

<u>First lines</u>: "The ostrich is the giant amongst living birds, the full-grown male standing some 8 feet high, and weighing about 300 lbs. It is flightless, the wings being smaller in proportion to the size of the body."

<u>Last line</u>: "The dainty, mincing step of the ostrich is a delight to watch, and, thanks to the Zoological Gardens, this can be done even in smoky London."

The first two lines explain that it is flightless. The last line explains that it is interesting to watch.

Supporting Ideas Questions

What are supporting idea questions asking?

Supporting idea questions ask for a piece of information that is explicitly stated in the passage.

Here are some examples:

1. The author describes…
2. According to the passage …
3. The passage provides information to support which statement?

Where should I look?

The answers to supporting idea questions are directly stated in the passage! All you have to do is find it! The first sentence of each paragraph tells you what that paragraph will be about. If you used the 2-1-2 strategy, you should have an idea of which topic is covered in each paragraph. Look at the paragraph that aligns with the topic in the question

✏ Try it!

Now, try it with these questions. For this practice, you do NOT need to read the passage first. Simply use the passage to find your answer.

1. According to the passage, which periodical did Thoreau contribute to?
   A. *The Lily*
   B. *The Dial*
   C. Ralph Waldo Emerson's paper
   D. Elizabeth Mallet's paper

Use this passage: (Don't read it. Just scan for the name Thoreau.)

1   In newspaper literature, women made their
2 entrance at an early period and in an important
3 manner. The first *daily* newspaper in the world
4 was established and edited by a woman, Elizabeth
5 Mallet, in London, in March 1702. It was
6 called *The Daily Courant*. In her salutatory, Mrs.
7 Mallet declared she had established her paper to
8 "spare the public at least half the impertinences
9 which the ordinary papers contain." Thus, the first
10 daily paper was made reformatory in its character
11 by its wise, woman founder.
12   The first newspaper printed in Rhode Island
13 was by Anna Franklin in 1732. She was a printer
14 to the colony, supplied blanks to the public
15 officers, published pamphlets, etc. In 1745 she
16 printed for the colonial government an edition of
17 the laws comprising three hundred and forty
18 pages.
19   Sarah Josepha Hale established a ladies'
20 magazine in Boston in 1827. She afterward moved
21 to Philadelphia, associating with Louis Godey,
22 and assuming the editorship of *Godey's Lady's*
23 *Book*. This magazine was followed by many
24 others, of which Mrs. Kirkland, Mrs. Osgood,
25 Mrs. Ellet, Mrs. Sigourney, and women of like
26 character were editors or contributors. These early
27 magazines published many steel and colored
28 engravings, not only of fashion but also
29 reproductions of works of art, giving the first

30 important impulse to the art of engraving in this
31 country.
32   Many other periodicals and papers by women
33 now appeared throughout the country. Mrs. Anne
34 Royal edited, for a quarter of a century, a paper
35 called *The Huntress*. In 1827 Lydia Maria Child
36 published a paper for children called *The Juvenile*
37 *Miscellany*, and in 1841 she assumed the
38 editorship of *The Anti-Slavery Standard*, in New
39 York, which she ably conducted for eight
40 years. *The Dial*, in Boston, a transcendental
41 quarterly, edited by Margaret Fuller, made its
42 appearance in 1840; its contributors, among
43 whom were Ralph Waldo Emerson, Bronson
44 Alcott, Theodore Parker, William H. Channing,
45 and the nature-loving Thoreau, were some of the
46 most profound thinkers of the time.
47   *The Lily*, a temperance monthly, was started
48 in Seneca Falls, N. Y., in 1849, by Amelia
49 Bloomer, the editor and publisher. It also
50 advocated women's rights and attained circulation
51 in nearly every state and territory of the Union.
52   In the United States the list of women's
53 fashion papers, with their women editors and
54 correspondents, is numerous. If the proverb that
55 "the pen is mightier than the sword" is true, a
56 woman's skill and force in using this mightier
57 weapon will soon change the destinies of the
58 world.

Explanation:

The correct answer is B - The Dial.

Here is where this is stated in the passage.
40 years. *The Dial*, in Boston, a transcendental
41 quarterly, edited by Margaret Fuller, made its
42 appearance in 1840; its contributors, among
43 whom were Ralph Waldo Emerson, Bronson
44 Alcott, Theodore Parker, William H. Channing,
45 and the nature-loving Thoreau, were some of the
46 most profound thinkers of the time.

---

2. According to the passage, when do ostriches use their wings?
    A. When turning abruptly
    B. When flying
    C. When running ahead at full speed
    D. When coming to a stop

1   The ostrich is the giant amongst living
2   birds, the full-grown male standing some 8 feet
3   high, and weighing about 300 lbs. It is
4   flightless, the wings being smaller, in
5   proportion to the size of the body. But the
6   energy that other birds employ in sustaining
7   flight, in the ostrich is instead expended in
8   running, so that it has reached a high degree of
9   speed—no less, in fact, than twenty-six miles
10 an hour.
11 When at full speed, it is generally
12 believed the ostrich derives no small help from
13 the wings, which are used sail-wise. Nor is this
14 belief by any means a modern one, for all of
15 us, must be familiar with Job's observations on
16 this subject: "What time she lifteth up her
17 wings on high, she scorneth the horse and his
18 rider." The wings are never used in running at
19 full speed, but are of much service in turning,
20 "enabling the bird to double abruptly, even
21 when going at top speed." In justice to the older
22 observers, however, it must be remarked that
23 ostriches do run with raised wings, but only at
24 the commencement of the run, or in covering a

25 short distance, when the pace may be
26 considerable; but if circumstances demand
27 "full speed ahead," they are held close to the
28 body, where they offer the least resistance to
29 speed.
30 With the gradual perfection of its
31 running powers, there has followed a gradual
32 change in the form of the leg. This change has
33 taken place by a reduction in the number of
34 toes. Of the original five with which its
35 ancestors began life only two now remain—the
36 third and fourth. The third is of great size,
37 having waxed great at the expense of the other
38 toes, a growth which seems to be still in
39 progress, since the fourth toe is undoubtedly
40 dwindling. It is very small and gives
41 unmistakable signs of growing smaller since it
42 has now become nailless. When it has quite
43 disappeared, the ostrich, like the horse, will
44 have but a single toe on each foot—the third.
45 The dainty, mincing step of the ostrich is a
46 delight to watch, and, thanks to the Zoological
47 Gardens, this can be done even in smoky
48 London.

Explanation:

The correct answer is A- When turning abruptly.

The second paragraph discusses the use of its wings. This sentence most clearly states the answer:
18 rider." The wings are never used in running at
19 full speed, but are of much service in turning,
20 "enabling the bird to double abruptly, even
21 when going at top speed." In justice to the older

---

3. Which of the following statements is best supported by the passage?
    A. Attention comes more easily to some than to others
    B. Attention requires us to disregard one matter and focus on another
    C. Many lectures are slow and difficult to pay attention to
    D. Our ability to pay attention is based on the development of our prefrontal cortex

1   It is by attention that we gather and mass
2   our mental energy upon the critical and
3   important points in our thinking. *The*
4   *concentration of the mind's energy on one*
5   *object of thought is attention.*
6   Everyone knows what it is to attend. A
7   story so fascinating that we cannot leave it,
8   the critical points in a game, an interesting
9   sermon or lecture, a sparkling conversation—
10 all these compel our attention. So completely
11 is our mind's energy centered on them and
12 withdrawn from other things that we are
13 scarcely aware of what is going on about us.
14 We are also familiar with another kind of
15 attention. We all have read a dull story,
16 watched a slow game, listened to a lecture or
17 sermon that drags, and taken part in a
18 conversation that was a bore. We gave these
19 things our attention, but only with effort. Our
20 mind's energy seemed to center on anything
21 rather than the matter at hand. A thousand
22

23 objects from outside enticed us away, and it
24 required the frequent "mental jerk" to bring us
25 to the subject at hand. And when brought
26 back to our thought problem we felt the
27 constant "tug" of mind to be free again.
28 But this very effort of the mind to free
29 itself from one object of thought that it may
30 busy itself with another is *because attention is*
31 *solicited by this other*. Some object in our
32 field of consciousness is always exerting an
33 appeal for attention, and to attend *to* one thing
34 is always to attend *away from* a multitude of
35 other things upon which the thought might
36 rest. We may therefore say that attention is
37 constantly *selecting* in our stream of thought
38 those aspects that are to receive emphasis and
39 consideration. From moment to moment it
40 determines the points at which our mental
41 energy shall be centered.

Explanation:

The correct answer is B - Attention requires us to disregard one matter and focus on another

28   But this very effort of the mind to free
29 itself from one object of thought that it may
30 busy itself with another is *because attention is*
31 *solicited by this other*. Some object in our
32 field of consciousness is always exerting an
33 appeal for attention, and to attend *to* one thing
34 is always to attend *away from* a multitude of
35 other things upon which the thought might
36 rest. We may therefore say that attention is

---

4. According to the passage, when is aqueous lava produced?
   A. When an active volcano erupts
   B. When lava hardens
   C. When a previously extinct volcano becomes active
   D. When a crater lake is formed

Use this passage:

1 A volcano that throws out molten rock, vapor, and
2 gases is known as an *active volcano*. An active
3 volcano, however, is only correctly said to be in a
4 state of eruption when the quantity of the molten
5 rock, lava, or vapor it throws out greatly exceeds
6 the ordinary amount.
7   Sometimes the volcanic activity so greatly
8 decreases that the molten rock or lava no longer
9 rises in the crater, but, on the contrary, begins to
10 sink. The lava then begins to harden on the surface,
11 and, if the time is sufficient, the hardened part
12 extends for a considerable distance downward. In
13 this way the opening connecting the crater with the
14 molten lava below becomes gradually closed, the
15 volcano being thus shut up, or corked, just as a
16 bottle is tightly closed using a cork driven into the
17 opening at its top to prevent the escape of the liquid
18 it contains. A volcano thus choked or corked up is
19 said to be *extinct*.
20   When we speak of an extinct volcano, we
21 do not mean that the volcano will never again
22 become active. A volcano does not cease to erupt
23 because there are no more molten materials in the
24 earth to escape, but simply because its cork or crust
25 of hardened lava has been driven in so tightly that
26 the chances of its ever being loosened again seem
27 to be very small. But small as the chances may

28 seem we must not forget that the volcano may at
29 any time become active or go into its old business
30 of throwing out materials through its crater.
31   Since the plug of hardened lava in the
32 volcanic crater is generally at a much lower level
33 than the top of the crater, the crater will soon
34 become filled to a greater or lesser depth with
35 water, produced either by the rain or by the melting
36 of the snow that falls on the top of the mountain.
37 Crater lakes, often of very great depths, are
38 common in extinct volcanoes.
39   Of course, when an extinct volcano again
40 becomes active, two things must happen if the
41 eruption is explosive. In the first place, the force of
42 the explosion must be sufficiently great to loosen
43 the stopper or plug of hardened lava which stops it.
44 But besides the breaking up of the stopper, the lake
45 in the crater of the volcano is thrown out along with
46 the cinders or ashes, producing very destructive
47 flows of what are called aqueous lava or mud
48 streams. These streams flow down the sides of the
49 mountain, carrying with them immense quantities
50 of both the ashes thrown out during the eruption, or
51 those that have collected around the sides of the
52 crater during previous eruptions. Very frequently,
53 these streams of aqueous lava produce greater
54 destruction than the molten lava.

Explanation:

The correct answer is C. This paragraph discusses what happens when an extinct volcano erupts, including the production of aqueous lava.

39   Of course, when an extinct volcano again
40 becomes active, two things must happen if the
41 eruption is explosive. In the first place, the force of
42 the explosion must be sufficiently great to loosen
43 the stopper or plug of hardened lava which stops it.
44 But besides the breaking up of the stopper, the lake
45 in the crater of the volcano is thrown out along with
46 the cinders or ashes, producing very destructive
47 flows of what are called aqueous lava or mud
48 streams. These streams flow down the sides of the
49 mountain, carrying with them immense quantities
50 of both the ashes thrown out during the eruption, or
51 those that have collected around the sides of the
52 crater during previous eruptions. Very frequently,
53 these streams of aqueous lava produce greater
54 destruction than the molten lava.

Vocabulary Questions

What are vocabulary questions asking?

Vocabulary questions ask you to define a word based on the context of the passage. Be careful! Many of the answer choices will include words that are accurate definitions of the given word. However, you need to determine the meaning based on how it is used in the passage.

Here are some examples:

1. In line "___", _____ most nearly means....
2. In line "___", the word _____ is used to mean....

Where should I look?

The question will give you the line that includes the word. Read the full sentence that includes that word. If you aren't sure about the meaning, you can also try reading the sentence before or after.

Remember, take your own guess for what the word means in the sentence before looking at the answers.

If you are unsure, try putting the options into the phrase as a replacement for the vocabulary word.

Try it!

Now, try it with these questions. For this practice, you do NOT need to read the passage first. Simply use the passage to find your answer.

1. In line 29, the phrase "old business" refers to...
   A. Becoming extinct
   B. Returning to an ancient state
   C. Erupting
   D. Returning to its usual state

Use this passage:

1   A volcano that throws out molten rock,
2 vapor, and gases is known as an *active volcano*. An
3 active volcano, however, is only correctly said to
4 be in a state of eruption when the quantity of the
5 molten rock, lava, or vapor it throws out greatly
6 exceeds the ordinary amount.
7   Sometimes the volcanic activity so greatly
8 decreases that the molten rock or lava no longer
9 rises in the crater, but, on the contrary, begins to
10 sink. The lava then begins to harden on the surface,
11 and, if the time is sufficient, the hardened part
12 extends for a considerable distance downward. In
13 this way the opening connecting the crater with the
14 molten lava below becomes gradually closed, the
15 volcano being thus shut up, or corked, just as a
16 bottle is tightly closed using a cork driven into the
17 opening at its top to prevent the escape of the liquid
18 it contains. A volcano thus choked or corked up is
19 said to be *extinct*.
20   When we speak of an extinct volcano, we
21 do not mean that the volcano will never again
22 become active. A volcano does not cease to erupt
23 because there are no more molten materials in the
24 earth to escape, but simply because its cork or crust
25 of hardened lava has been driven in so tightly that
26 the chances of its ever being loosened again seem
27 to be very small. But small as the chances may

28 seem we must not forget that the volcano may at
29 any time become active or go into its old business
30 of throwing out materials through its crater.
31   Since the plug of hardened lava in the
32 volcanic crater is generally at a much lower level
33 than the top of the crater, the crater will soon
34 become filled to a greater or lesser depth with
35 water, produced either by the rain or by the melting
36 of the snow that falls on the top of the mountain.
37 Crater lakes, often of very great depths, are
38 common in extinct volcanoes.
39   Of course, when an extinct volcano again
40 becomes active, two things must happen if the
41 eruption is explosive. In the first place, the force of
42 the explosion must be sufficiently great to loosen
43 the stopper or plug of hardened lava which stops it.
44 But besides the breaking up of the stopper, the lake
45 in the crater of the volcano is thrown out along with
46 the cinders or ashes, producing very destructive
47 flows of what are called aqueous lava or mud
48 streams. These streams flow down the sides of the
49 mountain, carrying with them immense quantities
50 of both the ashes thrown out during the eruption, or
51 those that have collected around the sides of the
52 crater during previous eruptions. Very frequently,
53 these streams of aqueous lava produce greater
54 destruction than the molten lava.

Explanation:

The correct answer is C – Erupting

"But small as the chances may seem we must not forget that the volcano may at any time become active or go into its **old business** of throwing out materials through its crater."

Here, "old business" means erupting since it says it is becoming active and throwing out materials through its crater.

---

2. In line 24, the phrase "mental jerk," most nearly means...
   A. A tug
   B. A rude and difficult person
   C. A forceful redirection of your own attention
   D. A thoughtful redirection of another individual's attention

Use this passage:

1   It is by attention that we gather and mass
2 our mental energy upon the critical and
3 important points in our thinking. *The*
4 *concentration of the mind's energy on one*
5 *object of thought is attention.*
6   Everyone knows what it is to attend. A
7 story so fascinating that we cannot leave it,
8 the critical points in a game, an interesting
9 sermon or lecture, a sparkling conversation—
10 all these compel our attention. So completely
11 is our mind's energy centered on them and
12 withdrawn from other things that we are
13 scarcely aware of what is going on about us.
14   We are also familiar with another kind of
15 attention. We all have read a dull story,
16 watched a slow game, listened to a lecture or
17 sermon that drags, and taken part in a
18 conversation that was a bore. We gave these
19 things our attention, but only with effort. Our
20 mind's energy seemed to center on anything
21 rather than the matter at hand. A thousand
22

23 objects from outside enticed us away, and it
24 required the frequent "mental jerk" to bring us
25 to the subject at hand. And when brought
26 back to our thought problem we felt the
27 constant "tug" of mind to be free again.
28   But this very effort of the mind to free
29 itself from one object of thought that it may
30 busy itself with another is *because attention is*
31 *solicited by this other*. Some object in our
32 field of consciousness is always exerting an
33 appeal for attention, and to attend *to* one thing
34 is always to attend *away from* a multitude of
35 other things upon which the thought might
36 rest. We may therefore say that attention is
37 constantly *selecting* in our stream of thought
38 those aspects that are to receive emphasis and
39 consideration. From moment to moment it
40 determines the points at which our mental
41 energy shall be centered.

---

3. As used in line 9, the word "impertinence" most nearly means...
    A. Modesty
    B. Impropriety
    C. Reforming
    D. Improvisation

1　　In newspaper literature, women made
2　their entrance at an early period and in an
3　important manner. The first *daily* newspaper
4　in the world was established and edited by a
5　woman, Elizabeth Mallet, in London, in
6　March 1702. It was called *The Daily Courant*.
7　In her salutatory, Mrs. Mallet declared she
8　had established her paper to "spare the public
9　at least half the impertinences which the
10　ordinary papers contain." Thus, the first daily
11　paper was made reformatory in character by
12　its wise, woman founder.
13　　The first newspaper printed in Rhode
14　Island was by Anna Franklin in 1732. She
15　was a printer to the colony, supplied blanks to
16　the public officers, published pamphlets, etc.
17　In 1745 she printed for the colonial
18　government an edition of the laws comprising
19　three hundred and forty pages.
20　　Sarah Josepha Hale established a ladies'
21　magazine in Boston in 1827.She afterward
22　moved to Philadelphia, associating with Louis
23　Godey, and assuming the editorship
24　of *Godey's Lady's Book*. This magazine was
25　followed by many others, of which Mrs.
26　Kirkland, Mrs. Osgood, Mrs. Ellet, Mrs.
27　Sigourney, and women of like character were
28　editors or contributors. These early magazines
29　published many steel and colored engravings,
30　not only of fashion, but also reproductions of

31　works of art, giving the first important
32　impulse to the art of engraving in this country.
33　　Many other periodicals and papers by
34　women now appeared throughout the country.
35　Mrs. Anne Royal edited, for a quarter of a
36　century, a paper called *The Huntress*. In 1827
37　Lydia Maria Child published a paper for
38　children called *The Juvenile Miscellany*, and
39　in 1841 she assumed the editorship of *The*
40　*Anti-Slavery Standard*, in New York, which
41　she ably conducted for eight years. *The Dial*,
42　in Boston, a transcendental quarterly, edited
43　by Margaret Fuller, made its appearance in
44　1840; its contributors, among whom were
45　Ralph Waldo Emerson, Bronson Alcott,
46　Theodore Parker, William H. Channing, and
47　the nature-loving Thoreau, were some of the
48　most profound thinkers of the time.
49　　*The Lily*, a temperance monthly, was
50　started in Seneca Falls, N. Y., in 1849, by
51　Amelia Bloomer, the editor and publisher. It
52　also advocated women's rights and attained
53　circulation in nearly every state and territory
54　of the Union.
55　　In the United States the list of women's
56　fashion papers, with their women editors and
57　correspondents, is numerous. If the proverb
58　that "the pen is mightier than the sword" is
59　true, a woman's skill and force in using this
60　mightier weapon will soon change the destiny
61　of the world.

"In her opening, Mrs. Mallet declared she had established her paper to "spare the public of at least half of the **impertinences** which ordinary papers contain."

A guess for this one could be rudeness or rude phrases and words.

Impropriety is the closest fit.

---

4. In line 37, the word "expense" most nearly means...
   A. Charge
   B. Detriment
   C. Injury
   D. Despair

1   The ostrich is the giant amongst living
2 birds, the full-grown male standing some 8 feet
3 high, and weighing about 300 lbs. It is
4 flightless, the wings being smaller, in
5 proportion to the size of the body. But the
6 energy that other birds employ in sustaining
7 flight, in the ostrich is instead expended in
8 running, so that it has reached a high degree of
9 speed—no less, in fact, than twenty-six miles
10 an hour.
11   When at full speed, it is generally
12 believed the ostrich derives no small help from
13 the wings, which are used sail-wise. Nor is this
14 belief by any means a modern one, for all of us
15 must be familiar with Job's observations on
16 this subject: "What time she lifteth up her
17 wings on high, she scorneth the horse and his
18 rider." The wings are never used in running at
19 full speed, but are of much service in turning,
20 "enabling the bird to double abruptly, even
21 when going at top speed." In justice to the older
22 observers, however, it must be remarked that
23 ostriches do run with raised wings, but only at
24 the commencement of the run, or in covering a

25 short distance, when the pace may be
26 considerable; but if circumstances demand
27 "full speed ahead," they are held close to the
28 body, where they offer the least resistance to
29 speed.
30   With the gradual perfection of its
31 running powers, there has followed a gradual
32 change in the form of the leg. This change has
33 taken place by a reduction in the number of
34 toes. Of the original five with which its
35 ancestors began life only two now remain—the
36 third and fourth. The third is of great size,
37 having waxed great at the expense of the other
38 toes, a growth which seems to be still in
39 progress, since the fourth toe is undoubtedly
40 dwindling. It is very small and gives
41 unmistakable signs of growing smaller since it
42 has now become nailless. When it has quite
43 disappeared, the ostrich, like the horse, will
44 have but a single toe on each foot—the third.
45 The dainty, mincing step of the ostrich is a
46 delight to watch, and, thanks to the Zoological
47 Gardens, this can be done even in smoky
48 London.

Explanation:

The correct answer is B – Detriment.

"The third is of great size, having waxed great at the **expense** of the other toes, a growth which seems to be still in progress, since the fourth toe is undoubtedly dwindling."

This is saying that the third toe grew making the others dwindle or become smaller. Thus, it is at the detriment of the other toes.

<u>*Detriment*</u>*: Drawback or disadvantage*

<u>*Hint:*</u> *If you don't know the meaning of an answer choice, try the other answer choices in the phrase. If none of them work, choose the word you don't know.*

Tone Questions

 ## What are tone questions asking?

Tone questions ask you to define how the author seems to feel about the subject.

Here are some examples:

1. Which word best describes the author's tone?
2. The author's tone when describing the topic can be best described as...
3. Which sentence best describes the author's attitude toward the topic?

 ## Where should I look?

Look at the first sentence and last sentence of the passage.

HINT: When in doubt, choose admiring or something similar if it seems generally positive. By writing a whole passage describing something in detail, authors are often showing admiration for what they are writing about.

✏ Try it!

Now, try it with these questions. For this practice, you do NOT need to read the passage first. Simply use the passage to find your answer.

1. Which of the following words best describes the author's attitude toward female writers?
   A. Skeptical
   B. Admiring
   C. Indifferent
   D. Optimistic

Use this passage:

1   In newspaper literature, women made
2 their entrance at an early period and in an
3 important manner. The first *daily* newspaper
4 in the world was established and edited by a
5 woman, Elizabeth Mallet, in London, in
6 March 1702. It was called *The Daily Courant.*
7 In her salutatory, Mrs. Mallet declared she
8 had established her paper to "spare the public
9 at least half the impertinences which the
10 ordinary papers contain." Thus, the first daily
11 paper was made reformatory in character by
12 its wise, woman founder.
13   The first newspaper printed in Rhode
14 Island was by Anna Franklin in 1732. She
15 was a printer to the colony, supplied blanks to
16 the public officers, published pamphlets, etc.
17 In 1745 she printed for the colonial
18 government an edition of the laws comprising
19 three hundred and forty pages.
20   Sarah Josepha Hale established a ladies'
21 magazine in Boston in 1827. She afterward
22 moved to Philadelphia, associating with Louis
23 Godey, and assuming the editorship
24 of *Godey's Lady's Book.* This magazine was
25 followed by many others, of which Mrs.
26 Kirkland, Mrs. Osgood, Mrs. Ellet, Mrs.
27 Sigourney, and women of like character were
28 editors or contributors. These early magazines
29 published many steel and colored engravings,
30 not only of fashion, but also reproductions of

31 works of art, giving the first important
32 impulse to the art of engraving in this country.
33   Many other periodicals and papers by
34 women now appeared throughout the country.
35 Mrs. Anne Royal edited, for a quarter of a
36 century, a paper called *The Huntress.* In 1827
37 Lydia Maria Child published a paper for
38 children called *The Juvenile Miscellany,* and
39 in 1841 she assumed the editorship of *The
40 Anti-Slavery Standard,* in New York, which
41 she ably conducted for eight years. *The Dial,*
42 in Boston, a transcendental quarterly, edited
43 by Margaret Fuller, made its appearance in
44 1840; its contributors, among whom were
45 Ralph Waldo Emerson, Bronson Alcott,
46 Theodore Parker, Wm. H. Channing, and the
47 nature-loving Thoreau, were some of the most
48 profound thinkers of the time.
49   *The Lily,* a temperance monthly, was
50 started in Seneca Falls, N. Y., in 1849, by
51 Amelia Bloomer, the editor and publisher. It
52 also advocated women's rights and attained
53 circulation in nearly every state and territory
54 of the Union.
55   In the United States the list of women's
56 fashion papers, with their women editors and
57 correspondents, is numerous. If the proverb
58 that "the pen is mightier than the sword" is
59 true, a woman's skill and force in using this
60 mightier weapon will soon change the destiny
61 of the world.

Explanation:

The correct answer is B – Admiring

<u>First line</u>: "In newspaper literature, women made their entrance at an early period and in an important manner."

<u>Last line</u>: "If the proverb that "the pen is mightier than the sword" is true, woman's skill and force in using this mightier weapon will soon change the destiny of the world."

The last line is very positive and shows that the author admires the female writers.

---

2. Which of the following best describes the author's tone?
   A. Indifferent
   B. Informational
   C. Hopeful
   D. Fearful

Use this passage:

1   A volcano that throws out molten rock,
2 vapor, and gases is known as an *active volcano*. An
3 active volcano, however, is only correctly said to
4 be in a state of eruption when the quantity of the
5 molten rock, lava, or vapor it throws out greatly
6 exceeds the ordinary amount.
7   Sometimes the volcanic activity so greatly
8 decreases that the molten rock or lava no longer
9 rises in the crater, but, on the contrary, begins to
10 sink. The lava then begins to harden on the surface,
11 and, if the time is sufficient, the hardened part
12 extends for a considerable distance downward. In
13 this way the opening connecting the crater with the
14 molten lava below becomes gradually closed, the
15 volcano being thus shut up, or corked, just as a
16 bottle is tightly closed using a cork driven into the
17 opening at its top to prevent the escape of the liquid
18 it contains. A volcano thus choked or corked up is
19 said to be *extinct*.
20   When we speak of an extinct volcano, we
21 do not mean that the volcano will never again
22 become active. A volcano does not cease to erupt
23 because there are no more molten materials in the
24 earth to escape, but simply because its cork or crust
25 of hardened lava has been driven in so tightly that
26 the chances of its ever being loosened again seem
27 to be very small. But small as the chances may

28 seem we must not forget that the volcano may at
29 any time become active or go into its old business
30 of throwing out materials through its crater.
31   Since the plug of hardened lava in the
32 volcanic crater is generally at a much lower level
33 than the top of the crater, the crater will soon
34 become filled to a greater or lesser depth with
35 water, produced either by the rain or by the melting
36 of the snow that falls on the top of the mountain.
37 Crater lakes, often of very great depths, are
38 common in extinct volcanoes.
39   Of course, when an extinct volcano again
40 becomes active, two things must happen if the
41 eruption is explosive. In the first place, the force of
42 the explosion must be sufficiently great to loosen
43 the stopper or plug of hardened lava which stops it.
44 But besides the breaking up of the stopper, the lake
45 in the crater of the volcano is thrown out along with
46 the cinders or ashes, producing very destructive
47 flows of what are called aqueous lava or mud
48 streams. These streams flow down the sides of the
49 mountain, carrying with them immense quantities
50 of both the ashes thrown out during the eruption, or
51 those that have collected around the sides of the
52 crater during previous eruptions. Very frequently,
53 these streams of aqueous lava produce greater
54 destruction than the molten lava.

Explanation:

The correct answer is B – Informational

<u>First line</u>: "A volcano that throws out molten rock, vapor, and gases is known as an *active volcano*."
<u>Last line</u>: "Very frequently, these streams of aqueous lava produce greater destruction than the molten lava."

---

3. In line 17, the word "drags" implies that the author's attitude toward the sermon or lecture would be...
    A. Disinterested
    B. Appreciative
    C. Outraged
    D. Hopeful

Use this passage:

1   It is by attention that we gather and mass
2   our mental energy upon the critical and
3   important points in our thinking. *The*
4   *concentration of the mind's energy on one*
5   *object of thought is attention.*
6   Everyone knows what it is to attend. A
7   story so fascinating that we cannot leave it,
8   the critical points in a game, an interesting
9   sermon or lecture, a sparkling conversation—
10 all these compel our attention. So completely
11 is our mind's energy centered on them and
12 withdrawn from other things that we are
13 scarcely aware of what is going on about us.
14 We are also familiar with another kind of
15 attention. We all have read a dull story,
16 watched a slow game, listened to a lecture or
17 sermon that drags, and taken part in a
18 conversation that was a bore. We gave these
19 things our attention, but only with effort. Our
20 mind's energy seemed to center on anything
21 rather than the matter at hand. A thousand
22

23 objects from outside enticed us away, and it
24 required the frequent "mental jerk" to bring us
25 to the subject at hand. And when brought
26 back to our thought problem we felt the
27 constant "tug" of mind to be free again.
28 But this very effort of the mind to free
29 itself from one object of thought that it may
30 busy itself with another is *because attention is*
31 *solicited by this other*. Some object in our
32 field of consciousness is always exerting an
33 appeal for attention and to attend *to* one thing
34 is always to attend *away from* a multitude of
35 other things upon which the thought might
36 rest. We may therefore say that attention is
37 constantly *selecting* in our stream of thought
38 those aspects that are to receive emphasis and
39 consideration. From moment to moment it
40 determines the points at which our mental
41 energy shall be centered.

Explanation:

The correct answer is A – disinterested.
"For we all have read a dull story, watched a slow game, listened to a lecture or sermon
that **drags,** and taken part in a conversation that was a bore."

In the context of the sentence, it is clear that the author would be bored. So, disinterested is correct.

---

4. Which of the following words best describes the author's attitude toward ostriches?
    A. Humorous
    B. Encouraging
    C. Admiring
    D. Apathetic

Use this passage:

1 The ostrich is the giant amongst living
2 birds, the full-grown male standing some 8 feet
3 high, and weighing about 300 lbs. It is
4 flightless, the wings being smaller, in
5 proportion to the size of the body. But the
6 energy that other birds employ in sustaining
7 flight, in the ostrich is instead expended in
8 running, so that it has reached a high degree of
9 speed—no less, in fact, than twenty-six miles
10 an hour.
11 When at full speed, it is generally
12 believed the ostrich derives no small help from
13 the wings, which are used sail-wise. Nor is this
14 belief by any means a modern one, for all of us
15 must be familiar with Job's observations on
16 this subject: "What time she lifteth up her
17 wings on high, she scorneth the horse and his
18 rider." The wings are never used in running at
19 full speed, but are of much service in turning,
20 "enabling the bird to double abruptly, even
21 when going at top speed." In justice to the older
22 observers, however, it must be remarked that
23 ostriches do run with raised wings, but only at
24 the commencement of the run, or in covering a

25 short distance, when the pace may be
26 considerable; but if circumstances demand
27 "full speed ahead," they are held close to the
28 body, where they offer the least resistance to
29 speed.
30 With the gradual perfection of its
31 running powers, there has followed a gradual
32 change in the form of the leg. This change has
33 taken place by a reduction in the number of
34 toes. Of the original five with which its
35 ancestors began life only two now remain—the
36 third and fourth. The third is of great size,
37 having waxed great at the expense of the other
38 toes, a growth which seems to be still in
39 progress, since the fourth toe is undoubtedly
40 dwindling. It is very small, and gives
41 unmistakable signs of growing smaller, since it
42 has now become nailless. When it has quite
43 disappeared, the ostrich, like the horse, will
44 have but a single toe on each foot—the third.
45 The dainty, mincing step of the ostrich is a
46 delight to watch, and, thanks to the Zoological
47 Gardens, this can be done even in smoky
48 London.

Explanation:

The correct answer is C – Admiring.

<u>First line</u>: "The ostrich is the giant amongst living birds, the full-grown male standing some 8 feet high, and weighing about 300 lbs."
<u>Last line</u>: "The dainty, mincing step of the ostrich is a delight to watch, and, thanks to the Zoological Gardens, this can be done even in smoky London."

The author says the ostrich is a "delight to watch," so the tone is admiring. Remember, when in doubt, choose admiring if the author is positive about the topic.

Organization Questions

What are organization questions asking?

Organization questions ask about how the passage is structured.

Here are some examples:

1. Which best describes the organization of the passage?
2. How is the passage structured?

Where should I look?

Unlike for other questions, first preview the answer choices. You should then look at the first line or two of the passage and the first line of each paragraph.

Keyword: *Chronological*

Chronological means that the information is in order of the time it occurred. A passage that is organized chronologically would explain what happened first, then what happened after, and so on.

 **Try it!**

Now, try it with these questions. For this practice, you do NOT need to read the passage first. Simply use the passage to find your answer.

1. Which best describes the organization of this passage?
   A. An argument is put forward and then refuted
   B. An opinion is presented, followed by an opposite opinion
   C. Facts and opinions are presented alternatively
   D. A phenomenon is explained through facts and definitions

Use this passage:

1 A volcano that throws out molten rock, vapor,
2 and gases is known as an *active volcano*. An active
3 volcano, however, is only correctly said to be in a
4 state of eruption when the quantity of the molten
5 rock, lava, or vapor it throws out greatly exceeds
6 the ordinary amount.
7   Sometimes the volcanic activity so greatly
8 decreases that the molten rock or lava no longer
9 rises in the crater, but, on the contrary, begins to
10 sink. The lava then begins to harden on the surface,
11 and, if the time is sufficient, the hardened part
12 extends for a considerable distance downward. In
13 this way the opening connecting the crater with the
14 molten lava below becomes gradually closed, the
15 volcano being thus shut up, or corked, just as a
16 bottle is tightly closed using a cork driven into the
17 opening at its top to prevent the escape of the liquid
18 it contains. A volcano thus choked or corked up is
19 said to be *extinct*.
20   When we speak of an extinct volcano, we
21 do not mean that the volcano will never again
22 become active. A volcano does not cease to erupt
23 because there are no more molten materials in the
24 earth to escape, but simply because its cork or crust
25 of hardened lava has been driven in so tightly that
26 the chances of its ever being loosened again seem
27 to be very small. But small as the chances may

28 seem we must not forget that the volcano may at
29 any time become active or go into its old business
30 of throwing out materials through its crater.
31   Since the plug of hardened lava in the
32 volcanic crater is generally at a much lower level
33 than the top of the crater, the crater will soon
34 become filled to a greater or less depth with water,
35 produced either by the rain, or by the melting of the
36 snow that falls on the top of the mountain. Crater
37 lakes, often of very great depths, are common in
38 extinct volcanoes.
39   Of course, when an extinct volcano again
40 becomes active, two things must happen if the
41 eruption is explosive. In the first place, the force of
42 the explosion must be sufficiently great to loosen
43 the stopper or plug of hardened lava which stops it.
44 But besides the breaking up of the stopper, the lake
45 in the crater of the volcano is thrown out along with
46 the cinders or ashes, producing very destructive
47 flows of what are called aqueous lava or mud
48 streams. These streams flow down the sides of the
49 mountain, carrying with them immense quantities
50 of both the ashes thrown out during the eruption, or
51 those that have collected around the sides of the
52 crater during previous eruptions. Very frequently,
53 these streams of aqueous lava produce greater
54 destruction than the molten lava.

Explanation:

The correct answer is D - A phenomenon is explained through facts and definitions.

First line: "A volcano that throws out molten rock, vapor, and gases is known as an *active volcano.* An active volcano, however, is only correctly said to be in a state of eruption when the quantity of the molten rock, lava, or vapor it throws out greatly exceeds the ordinary amount."

First line of each additional paragraph:

"Sometimes the volcanic activity so greatly decreases that the molten rock or lava no longer rises in the crater, but, on the contrary, begins to sink."

"When we speak of an extinct volcano, we do not mean that the volcano will never again become active."

"Of course, when an extinct volcano again becomes active, two things must happen if the eruption is explosive."

So, the volcanic activity is explained through an explanation of facts.

---

2. Which best describes the organization of this passage?
   A. A theory is presented and then refuted
   B. A process is presented step by step
   C. Several separate facts are followed by a general conclusion
   D. A term is defined, and its meaning is explained through examples and descriptions

Use this passage:

1   It is by attention that we gather and mass
2 our mental energy upon the critical and
3 important points in our thinking. *The*
4 *concentration of the mind's energy on one*
5 *object of thought is attention.*
6   Everyone knows what it is to attend. A
7 story so fascinating that we cannot leave it,
8 the critical points in a game, an interesting
9 sermon or lecture, a sparkling conversation—
10 all these compel our attention. So completely
11 is our mind's energy centered on them and
12 withdrawn from other things that we are
13 scarcely aware of what is going on about us.
14   We are also familiar with another kind of
15 attention. We all have read the dull story,
16 watched a slow game, listened to a lecture or
17 sermon that drags, and taken part in a
18 conversation that was a bore. We gave these
19 things our attention, but only with effort. Our
20 mind's energy seemed to center on anything
21 rather than the matter at hand. A thousand
22 objects from outside enticed us away, and it
23 required the frequent "mental jerk" to bring us
24 to the subject at hand. And when brought
25 back to our thought problem we felt the
26 constant "tug" of mind to be free again.
27   But this very effort of the mind to free
28 itself from one object of thought that it may
29 busy itself with another is *because attention is*
30 *solicited by this other*. Some object in our
31 field of consciousness is always exerting an
32 appeal for attention, and to attend *to* one thing
33 is always to attend *away from* a multitude of
34 other things upon which the thought might
35 rest. We may therefore say that attention is
36 constantly *selecting* in our stream of thought
37 those aspects that are to receive emphasis and
38 consideration. From moment to moment, it
39 determines the points at which our mental
40 energy shall be centered.

Explanation:

The correct answer is D - A term is defined, and its meaning is explained through examples and descriptions.

<u>First lines</u>: "It is by attention that we gather and mass our mental energy upon the critical and important points in our thinking. *The concentration of the mind's energy on one object of thought is attention.*"
<u>First line(s) of the next paragraphs (if the first line is really short you should read on a bit)</u>:
"Everyone knows what it is to attend. A story so fascinating that we cannot leave it, the critical points in a game, tan interesting sermon or lecture, a sparkling conversation"
"We are also familiar with another kind of attention. We all have read a dull story, watched a slow game…"
So, *"A term is defined and then explained through examples."*

---

3. Which best describes the organization of this passage?
    A. An argument is put forward and then refuted.
    B. A term is defined and explained with examples.
    C. A series of facts are presented to explain a curiosity.
    D. Two competing theories are proposed and debated.

Use this passage:

1 The ostrich is the giant amongst living
2 birds, the full-grown male standing some 8 feet
3 high, and weighing about 300 lbs. It is
4 flightless, the wings being smaller, in
5 proportion to the size of the body. But the
6 energy that other birds employ in sustaining
7 flight, in the ostrich is instead expended in
8 running, so that it has reached a high degree of
9 speed—no less, in fact, than twenty-six miles
10 an hour.
11 When at full speed, it is generally
12 believed the ostrich derives no small help from
13 the wings, which are used sail-wise. Nor is this
14 belief by any means a modern one, for all of us
15 must be familiar with Job's observations on
16 this subject: "What time she lifteth up her
17 wings on high, she scorneth the horse and his
18 rider." The wings are never used in running at
19 full speed, but are of much service in turning,
20 "enabling the bird to double abruptly, even
21 when going at top speed." In justice to the older
22 observers, however, it must be remarked that
23 ostriches do run with raised wings, but only at
24 the commencement of the run, or in covering a
25 short distance, when the pace may be
26 considerable; but if circumstances demand
27 "full speed ahead," they are held close to the
28 body, where they offer the least resistance to
29 speed.
30 With the gradual perfection of its
31 running powers, there has followed a gradual
32 change in the form of the leg. This change has
33 taken place by a reduction in the number of
34 toes. Of the original five with which its
35 ancestors began life only two now remain—the
36 third and fourth. The third is of great size,
37 having waxed great at the expense of the other
38 toes, a growth which seems to be still in
39 progress, since the fourth toe is undoubtedly
40 dwindling. It is very small and gives
41 unmistakable signs of growing smaller since it
42 has now become nailless. When it has quite
43 disappeared, the ostrich, like the horse, will
44 have but a single toe on each foot—the third.
45 The dainty, mincing step of the ostrich is a
46 delight to watch, and, thanks to the Zoological
47 Gardens, this can be done even in smoky
48 London.

Explanation:

The correct answer is C - A series of facts are presented to explain a curiosity.

First lines: "The Ostrich is the giant amongst living birds, the full-grown male standing some 8 feet high, and weighing about 300 lbs. It is flightless, the wings being smaller in proportion to the size of the body."

First line of each paragraph:
"When at full speed, it is generally believed the ostrich derives some help from the wings."
"With the gradual perfection of its running powers, there has followed a gradual change in the form of the leg."

No term is defined, and no argument is discussed or refuted in these sentences. So, the best answer would be a series of facts.

4. Which best describes the organization of this passage?
   A. From opinions to facts
   B. In chronological order
   C. From specific to general
   D. Different types of periodicals

Use this passage:

1   In newspaper literature, women made
2 their entrance at an early period and in an
3 important manner. The first *daily* newspaper
4 in the world was established and edited by a
5 woman, Elizabeth Mallet, in London, in
6 March 1702. It was called *The Daily Courant.*
7 In her salutatory, Mrs. Mallet declared she
8 had established her paper to "spare the public
9 at least half the impertinences which the
10 ordinary papers contain." Thus, the first daily
11 paper was made reformatory in character by
12 its wise, woman founder.
13   The first newspaper printed in Rhode
14 Island was by Anna Franklin in 1732. She
15 was a printer to the colony, supplied blanks to
16 the public officers, published pamphlets, etc.
17 In 1745 she printed for the colonial
18 government an edition of the laws comprising
19 three hundred and forty pages.
20   Sarah Josepha Hale established a ladies'
21 magazine in Boston in 1827. She afterward
22 moved to Philadelphia, associating with
23 herself Louis Godey, and assuming the
24 editorship of *Godey's Lady's Book.* This
25 magazine was followed by many others, of
26 which Mrs. Kirkland, Mrs. Osgood, Mrs.
27 Ellet, Mrs. Sigourney, and women of like
28 character were editors or contributors. These
29 early magazines published many steel and
30 colored engravings, not only of fashion, but
31 also reproductions of works of art, giving the

32 first important impulse to the art of engraving
33 in this country.
34   Many other periodicals and papers by
35 women now appeared throughout the country.
36 Mrs. Anne Royal edited, for a quarter of a
37 century, a paper called *The Huntress.* In 1827
38 Lydia Maria Child published a paper for
39 children called *The Juvenile Miscellany,* and
40 in 1841 she assumed the editorship of *The*
41 *Anti-Slavery Standard,* in New York, which
42 she ably conducted for eight years. *The Dial,*
43 in Boston, a transcendental quarterly, edited
44 by Margaret Fuller, made its appearance in
45 1840; its contributors, among whom were
46 Ralph Waldo Emerson, Bronson Alcott,
47 Theodore Parker, Wm. H. Channing, and the
48 nature-loving Thoreau, were some of the most
49 profound thinkers of the time.
50   *The Lily,* a temperance monthly, was
51 started in Seneca Falls, N. Y., in 1849, by
52 Amelia Bloomer, the editor and publisher. It
53 also advocated women's rights and attained
54 circulation in nearly every state and territory
55 of the Union.
56   In the United States the list of women's
57 fashion papers, with their women editors and
58 correspondents, is numerous. If the proverb
59 that "the pen is mightier than the sword" is
60 true, a woman's skill and force in using this
61 mightier weapon must soon change the
62 destiny of the world.

Explanation:

The correct answer is B – In chronological order

<u>First sentence</u>: "In newspaper literature, women made their entrance at an early period and in an important manner. The first *daily* newspaper in the world was established and edited by a woman, Elizabeth Mallet, in London, in March 1702. "

<u>First line of each paragraph</u>:
"The first newspaper printed in Rhode Island was by Anna Franklin in 1732."
"Sarah Josepha Hale established a ladies' magazine in Boston in 1827."
"Many other periodicals and papers by women now appeared throughout the country."
"The Lily, a temperance monthly, was started in Seneca Falls, N. Y., in 1849…"
"If the proverb that "the pen is mightier than the sword" is true,"

This shows that it is chronological since each paragraph is on a different time period and the dates are in order.

Inference Questions

What are inference questions asking?

Inference questions ask about information that isn't explicitly stated but is implied by the passage.

Here are some examples:

1. This passage implies...
2. What can you infer about...?

How should I solve them?

1. Rephrase the question in your own words so that it ends with a question mark. You may want to replace the word "infer" with "assume."
2. Find the section of the passage that discusses the topic.
3. Answer your rephrased question in your own words.
4. Check the answer choices.

 **Try it!**

Now, try it with these questions. For this practice, you do NOT need to read the passage first. Simply use the passage to find your answer.

1. The author implies that to pay attention to one thing, we must...
   A. Decide whether or not we have a true interest.
   B. Put in a significant amount of mental work and labor.
   C. Find a reason to question the topic at hand.
   D. Divert our attention away from many other things.

Use this passage:

1 It is by attention that we gather and mass
2 our mental energy upon the critical and
3 important points in our thinking. *The*
4 *concentration of the mind's energy on one*
5 *object of thought is attention.*
6   Everyone knows what it is to attend. A
7 story so fascinating that we cannot leave it,
8 the critical points in a game, an interesting
9 sermon or lecture, a sparkling conversation—
10 all these compel our attention. So completely
11 is our mind's energy centered on them and
12 withdrawn from other things that we are
13 scarcely aware of what is going on about us.
14   We are also familiar with another kind of
15 attention. We all have read a dull story,
16 watched a slow game, listened to a lecture or
17 sermon that drags, and taken part in a
18 conversation that was a bore. We gave these
19 things our attention, but only with effort. Our
20 mind's energy seemed to center on anything
21 rather than the matter at hand. A thousand
22

23 objects from outside enticed us away, and it
24 required the frequent "mental jerk" to bring us
25 to the subject at hand. And when brought
26 back to our thought problem we felt the
27 constant "tug" of mind to be free again.
28   But this very effort of the mind to free
29 itself from one object of thought that it may
30 busy itself with another is *because attention is*
31 *solicited by this other*. Some object in our
32 field of consciousness is always exerting an
33 appeal for attention, and to attend *to* one thing
34 is always to attend *away from* a multitude of
35 other things upon which the thought might
36 rest. We may therefore say that attention is
37 constantly *selecting* in our stream of thought
38 those aspects that are to receive emphasis and
39 consideration. From moment to moment, it
40 determines the points at which our mental
41 energy shall be centered.

Explanation:

The correct answer is D - Divert our attention away from many other things.

<u>Rephrase the question</u>: What do we have to do to pay attention to something?

<u>Answer in the passage</u>: Some object in our field of consciousness is always exerting an appeal for attention, and to attend *to* one thing is always to attend *away from* a multitude of other things upon which the thought might rest.

So, "divert our attention away from many other things."

---

2. This passage implies that the toes of ostriches have changed to…
   A. Improve their ability to run.
   B. Enable them to fly.
   C. Slow down their running.
   D. Reduce the likelihood of disease.

Use this passage:

1   The ostrich is the giant amongst living
2 birds, the full-grown male standing some 8 feet
3 high, and weighing about 300 lbs. It is
4 flightless, the wings being smaller, in
5 proportion to the size of the body. But the
6 energy that other birds employ in sustaining
7 flight, in the ostrich is instead expended in
8 running, so that it has reached a high degree of
9 speed—no less, in fact, than twenty-six miles
10 an hour.
11   When at full speed, it is generally
12 believed the ostrich derives no small help from
13 the wings, which are used sail-wise. Nor is this
14 belief by any means a modern one, for all of us
15 must be familiar with Job's observations on
16 this subject: "What time she lifteth up her
17 wings on high, she scorneth the horse and his
18 rider." The wings are never used in running at
19 full speed, but are of much service in turning,
20 "enabling the bird to double abruptly, even
21 when going at top speed." In justice to the older
22 observers, however, it must be remarked that
23 ostriches do run with raised wings, but only at
24 the commencement of the run, or in covering a

25 short distance, when the pace may be
26 considerable; but if circumstances demand
27 "full speed ahead," they are held close to the
28 body, where they offer the least resistance to
29 speed.
30   With the gradual perfection of its
31 running powers, there has followed a gradual
32 change in the form of the leg. This change has
33 taken place by a reduction in the number of
34 toes. Of the original five with which its
35 ancestors began life only two now remain—the
36 third and fourth. The third is of great size,
37 having waxed great at the expense of the other
38 toes, a growth which seems to be still in
39 progress, since the fourth toe is undoubtedly
40 dwindling. It is very small, and gives
41 unmistakable signs of growing smaller, since it
42 has now become nailless. When it has quite
43 disappeared, the ostrich, like the horse, will
44 have but a single toe on each foot—the third.
45 The dainty, mincing step of the ostrich is a
46 delight to watch, and, thanks to the Zoological
47 Gardens, this can be done even in smoky
48 London.

Explanation:

The correct answer is A – Improve their ability to run.

<u>Rephrase the question</u>: Why have ostrich toes changed?

<u>Answer in the passage</u>: "With the gradual perfection of its running powers, there has followed a gradual change in the form of the leg. This change has taken place by a reduction in the number of toes."

So, the answer is "Improve their ability to run."

---

3. By referencing the proverb in line 58, the author implies that...
   A. Women can write their arguments to make change instead of fighting in wars
   B. Women will change the world through their writing
   C. It would be better for women to fight in battle than to write in newspapers
   D. Newspapers are more effective than battles

Use this passage:

1   In newspaper literature, women made
2 their entrance at an early period and in an
3 important manner. The first *daily* newspaper
4 in the world was established and edited by a
5 woman, Elizabeth Mallet, in London, in
6 March 1702. It was called *The Daily Courant*.
7 In her salutatory, Mrs. Mallet declared she
8 had established her paper to "spare the public
9 at least half the impertinences which the
10 ordinary papers contain." Thus, the first daily
11 paper was made reformatory in character by
12 its wise, woman founder.
13   The first newspaper printed in Rhode
14 Island was by Anna Franklin in 1732. She
15 was a printer to the colony, supplied blanks to
16 the public officers, published pamphlets, etc.
17 In 1745 she printed for the colonial
18 government an edition of the laws comprising
19 three hundred and forty pages.
20   Sarah Josepha Hale established a ladies'
21 magazine in Boston in 1827.She afterward
22 moved to Philadelphia, associating with Louis
23 Godey, and assuming the editorship
24 of *Godey's Lady's Book*. This magazine was
25 followed by many others, of which Mrs.
26 Kirkland, Mrs. Osgood, Mrs. Ellet, Mrs.
27 Sigourney, and women of like character were
28 editors or contributors. These early magazines
29 published many steel and colored engravings,
30 not only of fashion, but also reproductions of

31 works of art, giving the first important
32 impulse to the art of engraving in this country.
33   Many other periodicals and papers by
34 women now appeared throughout the country.
35 Mrs. Anne Royal edited, for a quarter of a
36 century, a paper called *The Huntress*. In 1827
37 Lydia Maria Child published a paper for
38 children called *The Juvenile Miscellany*, and
39 in 1841 she assumed the editorship of *The*
40 *Anti-Slavery Standard*, in New York, which
41 she ably conducted for eight years. *The Dial*,
42 in Boston, a transcendental quarterly, edited
43 by Margaret Fuller, made its appearance in
44 1840; its contributors, among whom were
45 Ralph Waldo Emerson, Bronson Alcott,
46 Theodore Parker, Wm. H. Channing, and the
47 nature-loving Thoreau, were some of the most
48 profound thinkers of the time.
49   *The Lily*, a temperance monthly, was
50 started in Seneca Falls, N. Y., in 1849, by
51 Amelia Bloomer, the editor and publisher. It
52 also advocated women's rights and attained
53 circulation in nearly every state and territory
54 of the Union.
55   In the United States the list of women's
56 fashion papers, with their women editors and
57 correspondents, is numerous. If the proverb
58 that "the pen is mightier than the sword" is
59 true, a woman's skill and force in using this
60 mightier weapon will soon change the destiny
61 of the world.

Explanation:

The correct answer is B - Women will change the world through their writing.

Rephrase the question:
What does the author mean by the proverb "the pen is mightier than the sword?"

Answer in the passage:
If the proverb that "the pen is mightier than the sword" is true, a woman's skill and force in using this mightier weapon must soon change the destiny of the world.

So, "Women will change the world with their writing."

---

4. This passage supports which of the following statements
   A. Extinct volcanoes are not dangerous.
   B. A stopper in a volcano is most often broken by a human influence on the environment.
   C. Mud streams can cause damage when once-extinct volcanoes become active.
   D. Crater lakes are most often the result of active volcanoes erupting.

Use this passage:

1 A volcano that throws out molten rock,
2 vapor, and gases is known as an *active volcano*. An
3 active volcano, however, is only correctly said to
4 be in a state of eruption when the quantity of the
5 molten rock, lava, or vapor it throws out greatly
6 exceeds the ordinary amount.
7 Sometimes the volcanic activity so greatly
8 decreases that the molten rock or lava no longer
9 rises in the crater, but, on the contrary, begins to
10 sink. The lava then begins to harden on the surface,
11 and, if the time is sufficient, the hardened part
12 extends for a considerable distance downward. In
13 this way the opening connecting the crater with the
14 molten lava below becomes gradually closed, the
15 volcano being thus shut up, or corked, just as a
16 bottle is tightly closed using a cork driven into the
17 opening at its top to prevent the escape of the liquid
18 it contains. A volcano thus choked or corked up is
19 said to be *extinct*.
20 When we speak of an extinct volcano, we
21 do not mean that the volcano will never again
22 become active. A volcano does not cease to erupt
23 because there are no more molten materials in the
24 earth to escape, but simply because its cork or crust
25 of hardened lava has been driven in so tightly that
26 the chances of its ever being loosened again seem
27 to be very small. But small as the chances may

28 seem we must not forget that the volcano may at
29 any time become active or go into its old business
30 of throwing out materials through its crater.
31 Since the plug of hardened lava in the
32 volcanic crater is generally at a much lower level
33 than the top of the crater, the crater will soon
34 become filled to a greater or lesser depth with
35 water, produced either by the rain or by the melting
36 of the snow that falls on the top of the mountain.
37 Crater lakes, often of very great depths, are
38 common in extinct volcanoes.
39 Of course, when an extinct volcano again
40 becomes active, two things must happen if the
41 eruption is explosive. In the first place, the force of
42 the explosion must be sufficiently great to loosen
43 the stopper or plug of hardened lava which stops it.
44 But besides the breaking up of the stopper, the lake
45 in the crater of the volcano is thrown out along with
46 the cinders or ashes, producing very destructive
47 flows of what are called aqueous lava or mud
48 streams. These streams flow down the sides of the
49 mountain, carrying with them immense quantities
50 of both the ashes thrown out during the eruption, or
51 those that have collected around the sides of the
52 crater during previous eruptions. Very frequently,
53 these streams of aqueous lava produce greater
54 destruction than the molten lava.

Explanation:

The correct answer is C - Mud streams can cause damage when once-extinct volcanoes become active.

This question requires you to look at each option and decide if it is true or false –
    A. Extinct volcanoes are not dangerous.
<u>False-</u> The passage states that extinct volcanoes can erupt (which would be dangerous).

    B. A stopper in a volcano is most often broken by a human influence on the environment
<u>False-</u> Human impact on the environment is never discussed in the passage.

    C. **Mud streams can cause damage when once-extinct volcanoes become active**
<u>True</u> - " Of course, when an extinct volcano again becomes active, two things must happen if the eruption is explosive ...the lake in the crater of the volcano is thrown out along with the cinders or ashes, producing very destructive flows of what are called aqueous lava or mud streams."

    D. Crater lakes are most often the result of active volcanoes erupting.
<u>False-</u> "Crater lakes, often of very great depths, are common in extinct volcanoes. "

The Essay

Essay Strategies

Approaching the Prompt

1. Brainstorm ideas for potential answers to the question.

2. Choose an answer that you know a lot about.

3. Write a mini-outline with your topic and two to three key points (these are your body paragraphs).

4. Write a thesis that directly answers the prompt and includes your two to three reasons.

5. Write your essay!

Structuring the Essay

Introduction Paragraph

- 2-3 sentences
- Ends with your thesis statement

Body Paragraph 1 (first point)

- Topic Sentence
- Evidence
- Explanation
- Evidence
- Explanation
- Concluding Sentence

Body Paragraph 2 (second point)

- Topic Sentence
- Evidence
- Explanation
- Evidence
- Explanation
- Concluding Sentence

Body Paragraph 3 (third point – optional for middle level)

Conclusion

- 2-3 sentences
- Starts with a restatement of your thesis

Formatting and Editing Tips

- Indent each paragraph.

- Keep your introduction and conclusion sentence short (2-3 sentences).

- Don't use informal words.

  - you, we, stuff, thing, good, bad, huge

If you are writing by hand:

- Write the full essay prompt at the top of your page.

- Use a pen and write in print (not cursive).

- Add a big indent before each paragraph.

- Cross out mistakes with a line, don't scribble out.

Preparing for Common Essay Prompts

Most often, the ISEE essay prompts will fit into one of these five categories. Preparing for each of these categories can help you feel prepared on the day of the test.

A person of significance

Who is someone you admire? Why?
Who is your personal hero? Why?
What qualities are most important to you in a friend?

A place of significance

If you could travel anywhere, where would you travel and why?
If you could plan a field trip, where would you go and why?

A problem to solve

What is one problem you would like to solve in the world today / or one problem at your school? How would you solve it?
Should schools have uniforms?
Should schools ban cell phones?

A personal experience

Describe a lesson you learned this year.
Describe a challenge you recently overcame.

A plan

If you could write a book, what would it be about and why?
What career would you like to have one day? Why?
If you got $100, what would you do with it and why?

Plan for the Person of Significance Essay

Brainstorm!

Write as many ideas as you can think of! Who do you admire whom you know? Who do you admire whom you don't know but know a lot about?

Now, circle the ones you have the most to write about! If you choose someone you don't know, it is best to choose someone you know a lot about, otherwise, stick to someone you know.

Choose One:

Make a mini outline responding to this prompt:

Who is someone you admire and why?

Person:

Reason 1:

Reason 2:

Reason 3:

List specific facts and details you could use to support each reason.

If you don't have any facts or details for one of your reasons, change it!

Reason 1:

Reason 2:

Reason 3:

Write a practice thesis by completing this statement:

I admire _____ because _____,
(Reason 1)

_____, and _____.
(Reason 2)   (Reason 3)

Plan for the Place of Significance Essay

Brainstorm!

Write as many ideas as you can think of! What are your favorite places? Where do you want to visit? Where have you visited that you loved? Where could you take your class on a field trip?

Now, circle the ones you have the most to write about. It is okay if you say you want to visit a place you have already been. The most important part is that you know a lot about it.

Choose One:

Make a mini outline responding to this prompt:

If you could travel anywhere, where would you go and why?

Place:

Reason 1:

Reason 2:

Reason 3:

List specific facts and details you could use to support each reason.

If you don't have any facts or details for one of your reasons, change it!

Reason 1:

Reason 2:

Reason 3:

Write a practice thesis by completing this statement:

I would travel to _____ because
_____,
                                                 (Reason 1)

_____, and _____.

Plan for the Problem to Solve Essay

Brainstorm!

List problems in the world you would like to solve and how you would solve them.

List problems in your school you would like to solve and how you would solve them.

Sometimes, you are given a problem or key issue and asked to take a stand. Usually, this relates to school. Try these:

Should schools have uniforms?

Should schools ban cell phones?

Make a mini outline responding to this prompt:

What is one problem you would like to solve in the world today? How would you solve it?

Problem:

Why does this problem need to be solved?

How would you solve it?
    Part 1:

    Part 2:

Write a practice thesis by completing this statement:

_____ is a significant problem in the world because

_____; I would try to solve it by

_____, and _____.
        (Part 1)   (Part 2)

Make a mini outline responding to this prompt:

Should schools ban cell phones? Why or why not?

Yes or No:

Reason 1:

Reason 2:

Reason 3:

If you choose no, this paragraph should be about an alternative solution to the problem.

Write a practice thesis by completing this statement:

Schools _____ ban cell phones because of _____
      should or should not   Reason 1

_____, and _____.
              Reason 2   Reason 3

Plan for the Personal Experience Essay

Brainstorm!

What are some experiences that impacted you deeply? These may be positive ones or negative ones.

Choose Two:

What lessons did you learn?

Experience 1:

Experience 2:

Choose One:

Make a mini outline responding to this prompt:

What is an important lesson you have learned this year?

Lesson:

Experience you learned from:

How you learned from it:

Why it is important:

List specific facts and details you could use to support each reason.

Experience you learned from:

This should be a story or an event

How you learned from it:

There should be a key takeaway. Is there an example of how you applied that lesson?

Why it is important:

Why should people learn this lesson? Why did it matter to you?

Write a practice thesis by completing this statement:

This year, my experience _____ taught me

_____ because _____.

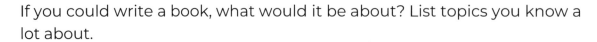 **Plan for the Future Plans Essay**

Brainstorm!

If you could write a book, what would it be about? List topics you know a lot about.

What career would you like to have one day? Choose something that relates to your school interests and something that you know about.

If you were given $100, what would you do with it? Think of ways you could use it to help others or to support your future.

Make a mini outline responding to this prompt:

If you could write a book, what would it be about? Why?

Topic:

Summarize the book:

Why would it be interesting?

Why would it matter to others?

Write a practice thesis by completing this statement:

If I could write a book, I would write about

_____

because_____,

and _____.

Make a mini outline responding to this prompt:

What career would you like to have one day? Why?

Career:

Why you are interested:

Why you would be good at it:

What you would do with it to help others:

Write a practice thesis by completing this statement:

I would like to be a _____ because _____

Paragraph 1

_____, and _____.

Paragraph 2   Paragraph 3

Make a mini outline responding to this prompt:

If you were given $100, what would you do with it and why?

Plan:

Reason 1:

Reason 2:

Reason 3:

Write a practice thesis by completing this statement:

If I were given $100, I would _____ because

_____, _____, and

       Paragraph 1   Paragraph 2

_____.

       Paragraph 3

Practice Tests

Practice Test # 1

Practice Test 1 – Verbal Reasoning

40 Questions – 20 Minutes

Part One—Synonyms

Directions: Select the word that is most nearly the same in meaning as the word in capital letters.

1. DILIGENT
   - (A) Destined
   - (B) Careless
   - (C) Challenging
   - (D) Hardworking

2. ADMONISH
   - (A) Applaud
   - (B) Banish
   - (C) Warn
   - (D) Flatter

3. EXPLOIT
   - (A) Manipulate
   - (B) Supply
   - (C) Protest
   - (D) Suffer

4. ASSERTIVE
   - (A) Soft
   - (B) Defeated
   - (C) Enduring
   - (D) Direct

5. FIDELITY
   - (A) Equality
   - (B) Extremely
   - (C) Loyalty
   - (D) Difficulty

6. INTROVERTED
   - (A) Energetic
   - (B) Reserved
   - (C) Confident
   - (D) Questioning

7. SENTIMENTAL
   - (A) Emotional
   - (B) Engaging
   - (C) Serious
   - (D) Generous

8. HYPOCRITE
   - (A) Mediator
   - (B) Lively
   - (C) Phony
   - (D) Genuine

9. BELITTLE

    (A) Criticize

    (B) Shrink

    (C) Believe

    (D) Annoy

10. GRACIOUS

    (A) Kind

    (B) Exciting

    (C) Faithful

    (D) Dishonest

11. OUTGOING

    (A) Blunt

    (B) Social

    (C) Formal

    (D) Shy

12. SNUB

    (A) Heat

    (B) Ignore

    (C) Encourage

    (D) Embrace

13. ROBUST

    (A) Willful

    (B) Flimsy

    (C) Haughty

    (D) Sturdy

14. INITIATE

    (A) Depart

    (B) Begin

    (C) Doubt

    (D) Ease

15. RESILIENT

    (A) Dense

    (B) Responsible

    (C) Strong

    (D) Animated

16. CORDIAL

    (A) Changeable

    (B) Polite

    (C) Subtle

    (D) Stubborn

17. VALIANT

    (A) Courageous

    (B) Evil

    (C) Weak

    (D) Supportive

18. HEADSTRONG

    (A) Athletic

    (B) Playful

    (C) Stubborn

    (D) Disorderly

19. STRENUOUS

    (A) Romantic

    (B) Protective

    (C) Straining

    (D) Dull

20. RETICENT

    (A) Pleasant

    (B) Timid

    (C) Guilty

    (D) Inspiring

Part Two—Sentence Completion

Directions: Select the word or word pair that best completes the sentence.

21. The researchers believed that the newly developed material could _____ up to 627° Celsius before melting.
    (A) Retract
    (B) Quadruple
    (C) Eliminate
    (D) Withstand

22. Pastor Marcus whipped the crowd up into a frenzy with a(n) _____ delivery of his Sunday-morning sermon.
    (A) Suspicious
    (B) Placid
    (C) Animated
    (D) Detrimental

23. In a bid to keep the truth from coming out, the once honorable judge dismissed the journalist's claims as nothing more than _____ lies and slander.
    (A) Frigid
    (B) Reserved
    (C) Malicious
    (D) Charming

24. After being sidelined in the nomination process for the Nobel prize, the renowned scientist became _____ at his loss.
    (A) Doubtful
    (B) Dejected
    (C) Heartened
    (D) Joyous

25. The team of engineers knew that it would be a great _____ to finish the project before the end of the quarter.
    (A) Optimism
    (B) Endangerment
    (C) Lapse
    (D) Accomplishment

26. Sir Davenport greeted the fair Lady May with a(n) _____ nod of his top hat and a pleasant, "Good morning."
    (A) Confident
    (B) Shameful
    (C) Courteous
    (D) Immature

27. While psychologists are still performing studies on the topic, research suggests that sons often try to _____ their fathers at a young age.
    (A) Enable
    (B) Emulate
    (C) Leave
    (D) Perspire

28. Zoologists have discovered that, despite being daring and adventurous by night, the Costa Rican margay is quite _____ by day.
    (A) Shaky
    (B) Bold
    (C) Boisterous
    (D) Apprehensive

29. Adolf Eichmann, a man known for organizing the Holocaust, was met with global _____ as his trial was broadcast from Jerusalem.
    - (A) Ambivalence
    - (B) Delight
    - (C) Disdain
    - (D) Indifference

30. Professor Davidson had always believed his lecture on plant immune systems was rather _____ but, judging by the number of sleeping students in his classroom, it must not have been.
    - (A) Advantageous
    - (B) Engaging
    - (C) Simplistic
    - (D) Boring

31. To establish themselves as a family-oriented business, the prospering start-up owners aimed to create a(n) _____ atmosphere for their workers.
    - (A) Congenial
    - (B) Preserving
    - (C) Chaotic
    - (D) Stifling

32. Although the federal government had promised to dedicate funds to the Navajo Nation, the money never came through, leading to anger in the community at the government's _____ to their needs.
    - (A) Indifference
    - (B) Accountability
    - (C) Generosity
    - (D) Responsiveness

33. Congressman William's push to pass laws without support from his voters led the people of his district to become _____ at his self-serving actions.
    - (A) Optimistic
    - (B) Drenched
    - (C) Satisfied
    - (D) Infuriated

34. When he failed to pass the final exam, James could not overcome the fear that his peers would _____ him for his failures.
    - (A) Overwhelm
    - (B) Dissect
    - (C) Mock
    - (D) Applaud

35. Michelle struggled to find a way out of her current _____ after losing her home in a fire but she kept her head up and pushed through.
    - (A) Flourish
    - (B) Refusal
    - (C) Predicament
    - (D) Perimeter

36. Here at the Sakha Riel Hotel, we aim to _____ our customers' every need to ensure that they have a pleasant and relaxing stay with us.
    - (A) Deny
    - (B) Praise
    - (C) Negotiate
    - (D) Accommodate

37. With a charming and agreeable personality, the once-unknown politician from Idaho quickly proved himself to be a _____ leader capable of bringing change to the system.
    (A) Dull
    (B) Charismatic
    (C) Chaotic
    (D) Foul

38. Following years of unkept promises, unfulfilled dreams, and a series of failed romances, the author previously known for his upbeat novels had become a _____.
    (A) Censor
    (B) Rookie
    (C) Diligent
    (D) Cynic

39. Though the art show received widespread positive reviews, one harsh critic complained that the _____ lighting was not strong enough to show the paintings at their best.
    (A) Bold
    (B) Soft
    (C) Brilliant
    (D) Deep

40. Finally, after years of conflict and legal disputes, the courts ruled to _____ the outdated policies requiring women to forfeit their property upon marriage.
    (A) Refrain
    (B) Overturn
    (C) Uphold
    (D) Withhold

Practice Test 1 – Reading Comprehension

36 Questions – 35 Minutes

Questions 1– 6:

1   It is an official thermometer's function to
2 indicate the air's true temperature. A
3 thermometer exposed to direct sunshine
4 records its own temperature—i.e., the
5 temperature of the glass and mercury—and
6 nothing else. A thermometer "in the shade"—
7 under a tree, for example—comes nearer to
8 showing the true air temperature. Still, it is
9 exposed to radiation from surrounding objects
10 and its readings will vary with the nature and
11 location of these objects.
12   A meteorological thermometer is nearly
13 always installed in a kind of latticed screen, or
14 shelter. It is thus largely protected from
15 radiation, while the air circulates freely
16 around it. Only when thermometers are
17 exposed under such standard conditions is it
18 possible to obtain comparable temperature
19 readings at different places, so that, for
20 instance, maps may be drawn showing the
21 distribution of this element over a country.
22   The best location for the thermometer
23 screen is a few feet above the sod. Many
24 thermometers of the United States Weather
25 Bureau are installed on the roofs of tall
26 buildings; not because this is an ideal
27 location, but because no better is available in
28 the heart of a large city, where, for practical
29 reasons, the office must be placed.
30   In many small towns, the site of the
31 station is such that the thermometer screen (or
32 "instrument shelter," as it is called in the
33 Weather Bureau) can be placed close to the
34 ground, and at the same time get ample
35 ventilation and be free from the radiation of
36 buildings. In certain large cities, the Bureau
37 maintains a branch station in a park or in the
38 suburbs, where satisfactory exposure for all
39 instruments can be secured.

1. Which statement best describes the main idea of the passage?

   (A) Thermometers take the temperature of the air.
   (B) Thermometers are installed on tall buildings for practical reasons.
   (C) Temperatures can be used to draw maps across different countries.
   (D) Ventilation is important when using thermometers.

2. In line 13, the phrase "latticed screen" most nearly means...

   (A) A special design used only in the United States.
   (B) A protected or enclosed area that houses the thermometer.
   (C) A park station where thermometers are housed in the suburbs.
   (D) The distribution of thermometers in a specific area.

3. The author identifies a true air temperature being taken in what conditions?

   (A) Direct sunlight
   (B) Rainy weather conditions
   (C) Protected from radiation
   (D) Early morning or late evening

4. How is the information organized in the article?

   (A) Stories are used to convey information.
   (B) Scientists explain different types of data.
   (C) A scientific instrument is identified and then its use is detailed.
   (D) The process for using a thermometer is explained step-by-step.

5. What issue does the article identify when considering where to place thermometers within a city?

   (A) The amount of people living in the city.
   (B) The number of animals that might interfere with the thermometer.
   (C) Finding a location where people can access it.
   (D) Space, a location with suitable exposure and proper conditions

6. The author describes the best location for a thermometer as what?

   (A) Covered, a few feet above the ground
   (B) The tallest building available in the city
   (C) In a place with a lot of people
   (D) Exposed to frequent radiation

Questions 7 – 12:

A sanctuary is a kind of wild "zoo," on a gigantic scale and under ideal conditions. As such, it appeals to everyone interested in animals, from the greatest zoologist to the holiday tourist. Before concluding I will show how worthwhile it would be to establish sanctuaries, even if they were not for people to enjoy the benefits.

The strongest of all arguments is that sanctuaries do not conflict with other interests, they actually further them. But unless we make these sanctuaries soon, we shall be disgracefully known, as the one generation that defrauded the livelihood of all the preservable wildlife that nature took a million years to evolve into its present beautiful perfection.

Only a certain amount of animal life can exist in a certain area, so the rest must go outside. Sanctuaries are more than wild "zoos", they are overflowing reservoirs, fed by their springs, and feeding streams of life at every outlet. They serve not only those interested in animal life but those who want to make sure animals are still available in the wild for hunting and food.

There are many instances of successful sanctuaries, permanent or temporary. For examples we have the Algonquin, Rocky Mountains, Yoho, Glacier, Jasper, and Laurentides in Canada; the Yellowstone, Yosemite, Grand Cañon, Olympus, and Superior in the United States. In addition, sanctuaries have proven successful with the sea lions of California, the wonderful revival of ibex in Spain, and deer in Maine, and New Brunswick, as well as on the great preserves in Uganda, India, and Ceylon. They have had positive effects on seafowl in cases as far apart in time and space as the Guano Islands under the Incas of Peru, Gardiner Island in the United States, and the Bass Rock off the coast of Scotland.

Yet I do not ignore the difficulties. First, there is the difficulty of introducing or enforcing laws for sanctuaries, since there have not been laws for them before. Next, there is the difficulty of arousing public opinion on any subject since some people misunderstand sanctuaries. We also must remember that if a protected species increases beyond its means, it may have to seek other kinds of food, which can sometimes have unfortunate results. However, with the right conditions, a sanctuary can help to support the decreasing population of animals.

7. Which sentence best expresses the main idea of the passage?

   (A) Wildlife sanctuaries act as "zoos" on a gigantic scale.
   (B) It would be worthwhile to establish wildlife sanctuaries.
   (C) The difficulties outweigh the benefits of establishing wildlife sanctuaries.
   (D) North American sanctuaries are superior to those found elsewhere.

8. The primary purpose of the fourth paragraph (lines 26-32) is to…

   (A) Ask for praise for the mentioned sanctuaries.
   (B) Highlight certain animals helped by sanctuaries around the world.
   (C) Show that sanctuaries can be successful after their establishment.
   (D) Show that the difficulties of creating sanctuaries can be overcome.

9. In line 14, the word "defrauded" most closely means…

   (A) Robbed.
   (B) Covered.
   (C) Saved.
   (D) Lied.

10. With which statement about sanctuaries would the author most likely agree?

    (A) Establishing sanctuaries requires more work than it is worth.
    (B) If a country has not established a sanctuary, it is because they probably do not have many wild animals.
    (C) Sanctuaries provide aid to both wild animals and people with special interests in wildlife.
    (D) Governments should be held responsible for pollution in sanctuaries.

11. The last two sentences of paragraph five (lines 49-55) imply that if a protected species grows too large…

    (A) The surplus must go outside the sanctuary.
    (B) The species can no longer be protected.
    (C) Other species will become threatened by the increase in protected species.
    (D) Protected species will not be able to find food and be at risk of extinction.

12. The author's tone in paragraph 4 (lines 26-42) can be described as

    (A) Humorous.
    (B) Doubtful.
    (C) Critical.
    (D) Optimistic.

1   When the American colonies began
2 their resistance to English tyranny, the women
3 — all this inherited tendency to freedom
4 surging in their veins — were as active,
5 earnest, determined, and self-sacrificing as the
6 men. Although, Mrs. Ellet in her "Women of
7 the Revolution" remarks, "political history
8 says but little, and that vaguely and
9 incidentally, of the women who bore their
10 part in the revolution," that does not show that
11 women had been as patriotic as men, and fully
12 embraced in the principles upon which the
13 struggle was based. Among the women who
14 manifested deep political insight, were Mercy
15 Otis Warren, Abigail Smith Adams, and
16 Hannah Lee Corbin; all closely related to the
17 foremost men of the Revolution.
18   Mrs. Warren was a sister of James
19 Otis, whose fiery words did so much to arouse
20 and intensify the feelings of the colonists
21 against British aggression. This brother and
22 sister were united to the end of their lives in a
23 friendship rendered firm and enduring by the
24 similarity of their intellects and political
25 views.
26 The home of Mrs. Warren was the resort of
27 patriotic spirits and the headquarters of the
28 rebellion. She wrote, "By the Plymouth
29 fireside were many political plans organized,
30 discussed, and digested." Her correspondence
31 with eminent men of the Revolution was
32 extensive and belongs to the history of the
33 country.
34   She was the first one who based the
35 struggle upon "inherent rights," a phrase that
36 afterward became a cornerstone of political
37 freedom. Mrs. Warren asserted that "inherent
38 rights" belonged to all mankind and had been
39 conferred on all by the God of nations." She
40 was connected with Thomas Jefferson, and
41 the Declaration of Independence shows the
42 influence of her mind. Among others who
43 sought her counsel upon political matters
44 were Samuel and John Adams, Dickinson
45 (that pure patriot of Pennsylvania), Jefferson,
46 Gerry, and Knox.
47   She was the first person who advised
48 separation from England and pressed these
49 views upon John Adams when he sought her
50 advice. At that time, even Washington had not
51 thought of the final independence of the
52 colonies. Mrs. Warren encouraged John
53 Adams to take bolder steps. Her advice was
54 not only sought in every emergency, but her
55 arguments also impacted the goals of political
56 parties. Mrs. Warren looked not to the
57 freedom of man alone, but to that of her sex
58 also.

13. The phrase "inherent rights" in lines 35-37 is meant to describe what?

    (A) Basic rights that all citizens should have
    (B) Powers found within all men and women
    (C) Rights that were given only to citizens who served the Revolution
    (D) Rights earned after indentured servitude

14. The main idea expressed in this passage can be explained as...

    (A) Men and women are equals in the eyes of the government.
    (B) Men are superior to women in all forms of government and leadership.
    (C) Women played an important role in the Revolution and had similar ambitions to their male counterparts.
    (D) Men negotiated the freedom of the colonies from the British Empire.

15. The term "cornerstone" in line 36 most nearly means...

    (A) The first stone when building a new structure.
    (B) An idea that contradicts prior arguments.
    (C) An important person.
    (D) An important ideology.

16. Which sentence best describes the organization of this text?

    (A) A biography of Mrs. Warren is told as a story.
    (B) An argument is supported by facts and a key historical example.
    (C) A chronological order of events of the Revolution is presented.
    (D) A list of specific facts relating to the Revolution is presented.

17. According to the text, which women had the power to influence the Revolution?

    (A) Women who were related to notable male revolutionaries.
    (B) British women who influence the aristocracy.
    (C) Women with a background in law.
    (D) Newly freed women.

18. The purpose of the last paragraph (lines 47-58) is to highlight what?

    (A) Mrs. Warren's influence on her male counterparts.
    (B) How the colonies acted against the British Empire.
    (C) Mrs. Warren's ability to debate and change the opinion of Washington.
    (D) The ability of John Adams to influence Washington.

1   To see a few impressions taken from a set
2 of woodblock prints or to print them oneself,
3 gives the best possible idea of the quality and
4 character of printmaking. So, also in
5 describing the work, it will perhaps tend to
6 make the various stages clearer if the final act
7 of printing is first explained.

8   The most striking characteristic of this
9 craft is the simplicity of the act of printing. No
10 press is required, and no machinery.

11   A block is laid flat on the table with its cut
12 surface uppermost and is kept steady by a
13 small wad of damp paper placed under each
14 corner. A pile of paper slightly damped and
15 ready for printing lies within reach just beyond
16 the woodblock, so that the printer may easily
17 lift the paper sheet-by-sheet onto the block as
18 it is required.

19   It is the practice in Japan to work squatting
20 on the floor, with the blocks and tools also on
21 the floor in front of the craftsman. In the West,
22 our habit of working at a table is less simple
23 but has some advantages. It is, however,
24 important to follow the Japanese practice of
25 handling the process with great care. No

26 description can give quite fully the sense of
27 extreme orderliness and careful deliberation of
28 their work. Everything is placed where it will
29 be most convenient for use, and this
30 orderliness is preserved throughout the day's
31 work. Their shapely tools and vessels
32 are handled with a deftness that shames our
33 clumsy ways, and everything that they use is
34 kept quite clean. This skillful orderliness is
35 essential to fine craftsmanship and is a sign of
36 mastery.

37   When printing on a table, the board lying
38 on the sheets of dampened paper is first moved
39 to the side so the sheets can be placed there
40 when they are done. If the block is dry, it is
41 thoroughly moistened with a damp sponge and
42 wiped. The color from a saucer is then brushed
43 over the printing surface thinly, and a trace of
44 paste is also brushed into the color. (This is
45 best done after the color is roughly spread on
46 the block.) The brush is laid down in its place
47 and the top sheet of paper from the pile is
48 immediately lifted on the block. This must be
49 done neatly, and it is important to waste no
50 time, as the color would soon dry on the
51 exposed block and print badly.

19. Which of the following artistic crafts does the passage most closely describe?

(A) Shodo; the Japanese art of calligraphy on silk or paper.
(B) Origami; the art of folding paper into shapes.
(C) Bonseki; the art of miniature landscapes.
(D) Ukiyo-e; the art of woodblock printing.

20. It can be implied from the passage that the "our" referred to in lines 22 and 32 refers to whom?

(A) Printers in training who are not yet skilled in the art
(B) American printers using more Western techniques
(C) Japanese masters who are now too old to carry on traditional methods
(D) Rival printers from China who wish to cast doubt on Japanese techniques

21. Based on the tone of the passage, how does the author view the technique described?

(A) Skeptically
(B) Admirably
(C) Curiously
(D) Hopelessly

22. "This," in line 48, refers to what step in the printing method?

(A) A trace of paste is brushed onto the color.
(B) The block is thoroughly moistened with a damp sponge and wiped.
(C) The brush is laid down in its place.
(D) The top sheet of paper is immediately lifted to the block.

23. The author would most likely agree with which of the following statements?

(A) The art form is primitive and undeveloped, not worth mentioning.
(B) Though squatting on the floor may seem unusual to Westerners, tea is best enjoyed in this posture.
(C) The art form is beautiful through its simplicity and precision.
(D) It is not necessary to see a final product to fully understand the quality of printmaking.

24. The word "deftness", as used in line 32, most closely means which of the following?

(A) Skillfulness
(B) Ignorance
(C) Awkwardness
(D) Deepness

1   Beautiful mineral deposits occur in
2 some natural caves. Deposits that look like
3 icicles are found hanging from the ceiling of a
4 cave. Other deposits jut upward from the
5 floor. In addition, some caves contain sheet-
6 like deposits spread along the ceiling, floor,
7 and walls. Calcite is one of the minerals that
8 commonly forms cave deposits.
9   Just a few of the caves in Texas
10 contain these deposits. They occur mostly in
11 the limestone rocks that are south and
12 southwest of the Llano uplift area of central
13 Texas. Some of the commercial caves that
14 contain good examples of calcite deposits are
15 located near Boerne in Kendall County and
16 near Sonora in Sutton County. Calcite
17 deposits also occur in Longhorn Cavern, a
18 large cave located in the Longhorn Cavern
19 State Park of Burnet County.
20   These caves were formed by
21 underground waters that moved through

22 cracks and pores in the limestone rocks and
23 dissolved passageways in them. After the
24 cave passages were made, water containing
25 dissolved calcium carbonate dripped into the
26 cave. As it evaporated, this water left behind a
27 deposit of calcium carbonate—the mineral
28 calcite.
29   You can better understand how the
30 cave deposits are formed by watching icicles
31 grow in wet, freezing weather. First, small
32 hanging drops of water freeze, and a small
33 icicle forms. Then, as more water drips over it
34 and freezes, the icicle grows longer and
35 wider. Some of the water drips completely
36 over the icicle and falls to the ground. There,
37 it either freezes into a sheet of ice, or begins
38 to build upward to form an upside-down
39 icicle. The water dripping down in the caves
40 evaporates instead of freezing, and in doing
41 so it leaves behind a deposit of calcite.
42

25. The main purpose of the passage is to explore…

(A) Various types of mineral deposits found in caves.
(B) Amateur cave exploration.
(C) The prevalence of limestone rocks in caves.
(D) Professional cave exploration by the oil and gas industry.

26. The text suggests examining what phenomenon to better understand the mineral deposits found in caves?

(A) Freshwater coral reef growth and bleaching.
(B) The growth and process of forming icicles.
(C) A map of natural and commercial caves found in Texas.
(D) Underground rivers.

27. What is the author's tone?

(A) Critical
(B) Optimistic
(C) Instructive
(D) Energetic

28. According to the text you could expect to find good Calcite deposits in which location?

(A) Kendall County
(B) Roger County
(C) Marshall County
(D) Plano County

29. In line 24, the term "passages" most nearly means?

(A) Towers
(B) Corridors
(C) Platforms
(D) Paragraphs

30. The organization of the passage most resembles which statement?

(A) Persuasive argument, the evidence is given to substantiate a conclusion.
(B) Timeline, the evidence is presented in chronological order.
(C) Competing storylines, telling two different, unrelated ideas.
(D) Presentation of various facts and information.

Questions 31 – 36:

1   When he was a low-paid lieutenant,
2 young Napoleon Bonaparte was very fond of
3 the "Lives of Historical Famous Men." But he
4 never tried to live up to the high standard of
5 character set by these historical heroes.

6   It will be very difficult to decide
7 whether Napoleon ever loved anyone besides
8 himself. He was respectful to his mother, but
9 she had the air and manners of a great lady, and
10 she knew how to command the respect of
11 children.

12   For a few years, Napoleon was fond of
13 Josephine, his pretty Creole wife, who was the
14 daughter of a French officer of Martinique and
15 the widow of the Vicomte de Beauharnais,
16 who had been executed by Robespierre when
17 he lost a battle against the Prussians. But the
18 Emperor divorced her when she failed to give
19 him a son and married the daughter of the
20 Austrian Emperor because it seemed good
21 policy.

22   During the siege of Toulon, where he
23 gained great fame as commander of a battery,
24 Napoleon studied Machiavelli with industrious
25 care. He followed the advice of Machiavelli
26 and never kept his word when he would benefit
27 from breaking it. The word "gratitude" did not
28 occur in his personal dictionary. But to be fair,
29 he did not expect gratitude from others either

30   He was totally indifferent to human
31 suffering. He executed prisoners of war (in
32 Egypt in 1798) who had been promised their
33 lives, and he quietly allowed his wounded in
34 Syria to be killed when he found it impossible
35 to transport them to his ships. He ordered the
36 Duke of Enghien to be sent to death and to shot
37 even though it was against all law and done just
38 because he thought that the "Bourbons needed
39 a warning." He ordered German officers who
40 were prisoners of war to be shot against the
41 nearest wall. Lastly, when a famous hero fell
42 into his hands after a most heroic resistance, he
43 was executed like a common traitor.

31. The fourth paragraph of the passage implies that, at the Siege of Toulon, Napoleon…

   (A) Helped to win a victory and became famous.
   (B) Was defeated and exiled to the Island of Elba.
   (C) Was a history student at the University of Toulon.
   (D) Showed that he could be as considerate as the "Historical Famous Men."

32. According to the passage, Napoleon respected his mother because she was…

   (A) Loving and gentle with all her children.
   (B) Careful to remain well-mannered and never raise her voice.
   (C) Knew how to demand the respect of children.
   (D) A great Italian woman, known for her gifted operatic singing.

33. Which sentence best states the main point of the fifth paragraph?

   (A) German officers captured while fighting should be shot against a wall.
   (B) Napoleon did not care about the suffering of other people.
   (C) The Duke of Enghein's execution was unfair and lacked legal backing.
   (D) Napoleon treated national heroes no different than common foot soldiers.

34. Which best describes the organization of this passage?

   (A) A claim is presented and then evidence is provided to prove that claim.
   (B) A claim is presented and then evidence is provided to argue against that claim.
   (C) Several facts are provided to detail a battle.
   (D) Several opposing opinions are discussed.

35. The passage supports which statement about Napoleon Bonaparte?

   (A) Bonaparte was a generous Emperor who cared for the people he ruled over.
   (B) Bonaparte preferred power over personal or emotional attachments.
   (C) Had Napoleon never read about the "Historical Famous Men" he would not have become Emperor.
   (D) Napoleon considered the lives of French soldiers more valuable than those of his enemies' soldiers.

36. The word "indifferent" as used in line 30, most closely means…

   (A) Passionate.
   (B) Conflicted.
   (C) Unconcerned.
   (D) Normal.

Practice Test 1 – Essay

Essay Topic:

What is a lesson you learned this past year? How did you learn it?

Write your essay in the space below:

_____

_____

_____

_____

_____

_____

_____

_____

_____

_____

_____

_____

_____

_____

_____

_____

_____

_____

_____

_____

_____

Practice Test 1 – Verbal Reasoning Answers

1. D	15. C	29. C
2. C	16. B	30. B
3. A	17. A	31. A
4. D	18. C	32. A
5. C	19. C	33. D
6. B	20. B	34. C
7. A	21. D	35. C
8. C	22. C	36. D
9. A	23. C	37. B
10. A	24. B	38. D
11. B	25. D	39. B
12. B	26. C	40. B
13. D	27. B	
14. B	28. D	

Practice Test 1 – Reading Comprehension Answers

1. A
2. B
3. C
4. C
5. D
6. A
7. B
8. C
9. A
10. C
11. C
12. D
13. A

14. C
15. D
16. B
17. A
18. A
19. D
20. B
21. B
22. D
23. C
24. A
25. A
26. B

27. C
28. A
29. B
30. D
31. A
32. C
33. B
34. A
35. B
36. C

Practice Test 1 – Reading Comprehension –
Where to Find the Answers

Passage 1:

1. **A - Thermometers take the temperature of the air.**

   1   It is an official thermometer's function to
   2   indicate the air's true temperature. A

2. **B - A protected or enclosed area that houses the thermometer.**

   13   always installed in a kind of latticed screen, or
   14   shelter. It is thus largely protected from

3. **C- Protected from radiation.**

   12   A meteorological thermometer is nearly
   13   always installed in a kind of latticed screen, or
   14   shelter. It is thus largely protected from
   15   radiation, while the air circulates freely
   16   around it. Only when thermometers are

4. **C - A scientific instrument is identified and then its use is detailed.**

   1   It is an official thermometer's function to
   2   indicate the air's true temperature. A

   12   A meteorological thermometer is nearly
   13   always installed in a kind of latticed screen, or

   22 |The best location for the thermometer
   23   screen is a few feet above the sod. Many

   30   In many small towns the site of the station
   31   is such that the thermometer screen (or
   32   "instrument shelter," as it is called in the

5. **D - Space, a location with suitable exposure and proper conditions.**

   26   buildings; not because this is an ideal
   27   location, but because no better is available in
   28   the heart of a large city, where, for practical
   29   reasons, the office must be placed.

6. **A - Covered, a few feet above the ground.**

   22   The best location for the thermometer
   23   screen is a few feet above the sod. Many

Passage 2:

7. **B- It would be worthwhile to establish wildlife sanctuaries.**

    1   A sanctuary is a kind of wild "zoo," on a
    2   gigantic scale and under ideal conditions. As

8. **C - Show that sanctuaries can be successful after their establishment.**

    26   There are many instances of successful
    27   sanctuaries, permanent or temporary. For

9. **A- Robbed.**

    11   they actually further them. But unless we make
    12   these   sanctuaries   soon,   we   shall   be
    13   disgracefully known, as the one generation that
    14   defrauded the livelihood of all the preservable
    15   wildlife that nature took a million years to
    16   evolve into its present beautiful perfection.

10. **C - Sanctuaries provide aid to both wild animals and people with special interests in wildlife.**

    22   outlet. They serve not only those interested in
    23   animal life but those who want to make sure
    24   animals are still available in the wild for hunting
    25   and food.

11. **C - Other species will become threatened by the increase in protected species.**

    49   sanctuaries. We also must remember that if a
    50   protected species increases beyond its means,
    51   it may have to seek other kinds of food, which
    52   can   sometimes   have   unfortunate   results.

12. **D – Optimistic.**

    26   There are many instances of successful
    27   sanctuaries,   permanent   or   temporary   For

    33   sanctuaries have proven successful with the
    34   sea lions of California, the wonderful revival
    35   of ibex in Spain, and deer in Maine, and New
    36   Brunswick, as well as on the great preserves in
    37   Uganda, India, and Ceylon. They have had
    38   positive effects on seafowl in cases as far apart

Passage 3:

13. A - Basic rights that all citizens should have.

34   She was the first one who based the
35 struggle upon "inherent rights," a phrase that
36 afterward became a cornerstone of political
37 freedom. Mrs. Warren asserted that "inherent
38 rights" belonged to all mankind and had been
39 conferred on all by the God of nations." She

14. C - Women played an important role in the Revolution and had similar ambitions to their male counterparts.

1   When the American colonies began
2 their resistance to English tyranny, the women
3 — all this inherited tendency to freedom
4 surging in their veins — were as active,
5 earnest, determined, and self-sacrificing as the
6 men. Although, Mrs. Ellet in her "Women of

15. D - An important ideology.

34   She was the first one who based the
35 struggle upon "inherent rights," a phrase that
36 afterward became a cornerstone of political
37 freedom. Mrs. Warren asserted that "inherent
38 rights" belonged to all mankind and had been
39 conferred on all by the God of nations." She

16. B – An argument is supported by facts and a key historical example.

1   When the American colonies began their
2 resistance to English tyranny, the women — all
3 this inherited tendency to freedom surging in
4 their veins — were as active, earnest,
5 determined, and self-sacrificing as the men.

18   Mrs. Warren was a sister of James Otis,
19 whose fiery words did so much to arouse and
20 intensify the feelings of the colonists against
21 British aggression. This brother and sister were

26   The home of Mrs. Warren was the resort of
27 patriotic spirits and the headquarters of the
28 rebellion. She wrote, "By the Plymouth

34   She was the first one who based the
35 struggle upon "inherent rights," a phrase that
36 afterward became a cornerstone of political
37 freedom. Mrs. Warren asserted that "inherent

47   She was the first person who advised
48 separation from England and pressed these
49 views upon John Adams when he sought her
50 advice. At that time, even Washington had not

17. A- Women who were related to notable male revolutionaries.

13 struggle was based. Among the women who
14 manifested deep political insight, were Mercy
15 Otis Warren, Abigail Smith Adams, and
16 Hannah Lee Corbin; all closely related to the
17 foremost men of the Revolution.

18. A - Mrs. Warren's influence on her male counterparts.

53 Adams to take bolder steps. Her advice was
54 not only sought in every emergency, but her
55 arguments also impacted the goals of political
56 parties. Mrs. Warren looked not to the
57 freedom of man alone, but to that of her sex
58 also.

133

Passage 4:

19. D - Ukiyo-e; the art of woodblock printing.

1   To see a few impressions taken from a set
2 of wood block prints or to print them oneself,

20. B - American printers using more Western techniques.

21 the floor in front of the craftsman. In the West,
22 our habit of working at a table is less simple
23 but has some advantages. It is, however,
24 important to follow the Japanese practice of
25 handling the process with great care. No

31 work. Their shapely tools and vessels
32 are handled with a deftness that shames our
33 clumsy ways, and everything that they use is
34 kept quite clean. This skillful orderliness is
35 essential to fine craftsmanship and is a sign of
36 mastery.

21. B - Admirably

1   To see a few impressions taken from a set
2 of wood block prints or to print them oneself,
3 gives the best possible idea of the quality and
4 character of printmaking. So, also in describing

8   The most striking characteristic of this craft

34 kept quite clean. This skillful orderliness is
35 essential to fine craftsmanship and is a sign of
36 mastery.

22. D - The top sheet of paper is immediately lifted to the block.

46 the block.) The brush is laid down in its place
47 and the top sheet of paper from the pile is
48 immediately lifted on the block. This must be

23. C - The art form is beautiful through its simplicity and precision.

8   The most striking characteristic of this
9 craft is the simplicity of the act of printing. No
10 press is required, and no machinery.

24. A - Skillfulness

31 work. Their shapely tools and vessels
32 are handled with a deftness that shames our
33 clumsy ways, and everything that they use is
34 kept quite clean. This skillful orderliness is
35 essential to fine craftsmanship and is a sign of
36 mastery.

Passage 5:

25. A - Various types of mineral deposits found in caves.

1   Beautiful mineral deposits occur in
2 some natural caves. Deposits that look like
3 icicles are found hanging from the ceiling of a
4 cave. Other deposits jut upward from the floor.

26. B - The growth and process of forming icicles.

29   You can better understand how the
30 cave deposits are formed by watching icicles
31 grow in wet, freezing weather. First, small
32 hanging drops of water freeze, and a small
33 icicle forms. Then, as more water drips over it

27. C – Instructive

1   Beautiful mineral deposits occur in
2 some natural caves. Deposits that look like
3 icicles are found hanging from the ceiling of a
4 cave. Other deposits jut upward from the
5 floor. In addition, some caves contain sheet-
6 like deposits spread along the ceiling, floor,
7 and walls. Calcite is one of the minerals that
8 commonly forms cave deposits.
9   Just a few of the caves in Texas
10 contain these deposits. They occur mostly in

28. A - Kendall County

13 Texas. Some of the commercial caves that
14 contain good examples of calcite deposits are
15 located near Boerne in Kendall County and

29. B – Corridors

22 cracks and pores in the limestone rocks and
23 dissolved passageways in them. After the
24 cave passages were made, water containing

30. D - Presentation of various facts and information.

1   Beautiful mineral deposits occur in
2 some natural caves. Deposits that look like

9   Just a few of the caves in Texas
10 contain these deposits. They occur mostly in

20   These caves were formed by
21 underground waters that moved through

Passage 6:

31. **A - Helped to win a victory and became famous.**

20   During the siege of Toulon, where he gained
21 great fame as commander of a battery, Napoleon

32. **C – Knew how to demand the respect of children.**

8 He was respectful to his mother, but she had the
9 air and manners of a great lady, and she knew
10 how to command the respect of children.

33. **B - Napoleon did not care about the suffering of other people.**

30   He was totally indifferent to human
31 suffering. He executed prisoners of war (in

34. **A - A claim is presented and then evidence is provided to prove that claim.**

1   When he was a low-paid lieutenant,
2 young Napoleon Bonaparte was very fond of
3 the "Lives of Historical Famous Men." But he
4 never tried to live up to the high standard of
5 character set by these historical heroes.

6   It will be very difficult to decide
7 whether Napoleon ever loved anyone besides
8 himself. He was respectful to his mother, but

30   He was totally indifferent to human
31 suffering. He executed prisoners of war (in

40 were prisoners of war to be shot against the
41 nearest wall. Lastly, when a famous hero fell
42 into his hands after a most heroic resistance, he
43 was executed like a common traitor.

35. **B - Bonaparte preferred power over personal or emotional attachments.**

6   It will be very difficult to decide
7 whether Napoleon ever loved anyone besides
8 himself. He was respectful to his mother, but

36. **C - Unconcerned**

30   He was totally indifferent to human
31 suffering. He executed prisoners of war (in
32 Egypt in 1798) who had been promised their
33 lives, and he quietly allowed his wounded in
34 Syria to be killed when he found it impossible
35 to transport them to his ships. He ordered the

Practice Test 1 – Essay Checklist

Introduction:

☐ The introduction paragraph is two to three sentences.

☐ The introduction paragraph ends with a thesis statement.

☐ The thesis statement responds to the questions and includes key reasons.

Body Paragraphs:

☐ The essay has two or three body paragraphs (three for upper level).

☐ Each body paragraph starts with a topic sentence.

☐ Each body paragraph has specific evidence.

Conclusion:

☐ The conclusion paragraph is two to three sentences.

☐ The conclusion paragraph starts with a restated thesis statement.

Overall Writing Quality:

☐ Each paragraph is indented.

☐ Writing is clear.

☐ Word choice is formal.

☐ The essay fully responds to the prompt.

☐ The essay shows positive qualities about the student. (Remember, the schools are reading it, and it is not given a score.)

Scoring Practice Test 1

Use this chart to approximate your percentile score based on your number of correct answers. The actual scoring is scaled based on the difficulty of the test you receive, so this is just an approximate score.

Middle Level

	# of Correct Answers	# of Correct Answers	# of Correct Answers
7th Grade Verbal Reasoning	21	26	32
7th Grade Reading Comprehension	19	25	31
8th Grade Verbal Reasoning	22	27	34
8th Grade Reading Comprehension	20	26	32
Percentile	25th	50th	75th

Upper Level

	# of Correct Answers	# of Correct Answers	# of Correct Answers
9th Grade Verbal Reasoning	23	29	35
9th Grade Reading Comprehension	22	28	33
10th Grade Verbal Reasoning	24	30	36
10th Grade Reading Comprehension	23	30	34
11th and 12th Grade Verbal Reasoning	25	32	37
11th and 12th Grade Reading Comprehension	24	31	35
Percentile	25th	50th	75th

Practice Test # 2

Practice Test 2 – Verbal Reasoning

40 Questions – 20 Minutes

Part One—Synonyms

Directions: Select the word that is most nearly the same in meaning as the word in capital letters.

1. SOLEMN

   (A) Stale

   (B) Somber

   (C) Frustrated

   (D) Generous

2. DENIGRATE

   (A) Criticize

   (B) Enhance

   (C) Estimate

   (D) Amaze

3. MEEK

   (A) Relinquish

   (B) Submissive

   (C) Resistant

   (D) Bold

4. SUCCINCT

   (A) Verbose

   (B) Concise

   (C) Insulting

   (D) Serious

5. AMELIORATE

   (A) Lessen

   (B) Strengthen

   (C) Build

   (D) Destroy

6. VEX

   (A) Annoy

   (B) Hope

   (C) Build

   (D) Belittle

7. NONCHALANT

   (A) Pleasant

   (B) Thorough

   (C) Unconcerned

   (D) Strict

8. COMPATIBLE

   (A) Agreeable

   (B) Improper

   (C) Conflicting

   (D) Complex

9. MOLLIFY

    (A) Irritate

    (B) Expand

    (C) Soothe

    (D) Excite

10. DESPAIR

    (A) Comfort

    (B) Misery

    (C) Ease

    (D) Patience

11. PLACID

    (A) Serene

    (B) Agitated

    (C) Wild

    (D) Orderly

12. ANIMOSITY

    (A) Respect

    (B) Sympathy

    (C) Hatred

    (D) Boredom

13. ORNATE

    (A) Dull

    (B) Decorated

    (C) Calm

    (D) Doubtful

14. PERCEPTIVE

    (A) Tough

    (B) Careless

    (C) Observant

    (D) Determined

15. COMMEND

    (A) Blame

    (B) Censure

    (C) Applaud

    (D) Cover

16. CONCUR

    (A) Agree

    (B) Refuse

    (C) Disjoin

    (D) Celebrate

17. AFFLUENT

    (A) Anxious

    (B) Wealthy

    (C) Impoverished

    (D) Friendly

18. PUGNACIOUS

    (A) Fearful

    (B) Playful

    (C) Argumentative

    (D) Kind

19. ADMIT

    (A) Confess

    (B) Absorb

    (C) Admonish

    (D) Accrue

20. Apex

    (A) Plateau

    (B) Morose

    (C) Peak

    (D) Bleak

Part Two—Sentence Completion

Directions: Select the word or word pair that best completes the sentence.

21. NASA's space shuttle fleet began setting records with its first launch on April 12, 1981, and continued to set high marks of _____ and endurance through 30 years of missions.
    - (A) Achievement
    - (B) Loss
    - (C) Optimism
    - (D) Surprise

22. My brother's _____ outlook on life did not even change when he won the million-dollar sweepstakes.
    - (A) Keen
    - (B) Morose
    - (C) Inquisitive
    - (D) Stable

23. Gorillas are gentle giants and _____ many human-like behaviors and emotions, such as laughter and sadness
    - (A) Exhibit
    - (B) Conceal
    - (C) Allow
    - (D) Charm

24. Although it seems _____ to use the weekends to do a major "catch-up" on sleep, it is actually counterproductive as it will make a person more tired.
    - (A) Useless
    - (B) Impractical
    - (C) Chaotic
    - (D) Enticing

25. The idea is to use technology not just to replace an existing service in a digital form, but to use technology to _____ that service into something significantly better and more advanced.
    - (A) Remove
    - (B) Stagnate
    - (C) Transform
    - (D) Recover

26. Teens spend a great portion of each day in school; however, they are unable to _____ the learning opportunities afforded by the education system, since sleep deprivation impairs their ability to be alert, pay attention, solve problems, cope with stress and retain information.
    - (A) Maximize
    - (B) Mutate
    - (C) Abridge
    - (D) Diminish

27. There is only one species of domestic horse, but around 400 different breeds that _____ in everything from pulling wagons to racing.
    (A) Hamper
    (B) Specialize
    (C) Excite
    (D) Bloom

28. Aria tried her hardest to _____ to the group of girls around her when she changed her hair and her wardrobe to fit in with the group.
    (A) Relay
    (B) Oppose
    (C) Ignore
    (D) Conform

29. With no expense spared, the 10,000 white flowers, 45 layers, and truffle garnish all contributed to a highly _____ cake.
    (A) Obsolete
    (B) Reasonable
    (C) Extravagant
    (D) Practical

30. Since I have a short attention span, I tend to read condensed stories instead of the _____ narratives on which they are based.
    (A) Terse
    (B) Notorious
    (C) Conclusive
    (D) Verbose

31. To get the job, Jane must find someone to _____ her as a good babysitter.
    (A) Endorse
    (B) Invalidate
    (C) Admonish
    (D) Repudiate

32. Whenever I smell something _____ coming from the kitchen, I know it is best to go to a friend's house for dinner.
    (A) Delectable
    (B) Peculiar
    (C) Tempting
    (D) Rowdy

33. Restaurants in the area are _____ with leftover food, throwing away thousands of pounds of fruit and vegetables every week
    (A) Cautious
    (B) Thrifty
    (C) Dismissive
    (D) Wasteful

34. Between 1850 and 1860, Tubman made 19 trips from the South to the North following the _____ known as the Underground Railroad.
    (A) Network
    (B) Interruption
    (C) Misery
    (D) Reel

35. Employees worked in teams to identify obstacles that may have _____ performance so that they could develop action plans to address these _____.
    - (A) Aided…. Problems
    - (B) Hindered…. Challenges
    - (C) Engaged…. Flaws
    - (D) Reimagined….Innovations

36. Ordinarily_____ and _____ places become beautiful and mystical when they are covered in a blanket of fresh snow.
    - (A) Mundane…. Dull
    - (B) Serene…. Ornate
    - (C) Unvaried…. Compelling
    - (D) Placid…. Coveted

37. Kyla was a/an _____ conversationalist, she showed so much _____ for her work and curiosity about the world around her.
    - (A) Exuberant…. Passion
    - (B) Avid…. Indifference
    - (C) Subdued…. Zeal
    - (D) Ebullient…. Disdain

38. Their _____ methods of manufacturing which made their processes _____and unpredictable made it seem as though they were stuck in the past.
    - (A) Innovative…. Slow
    - (B) Costly…. Expensive
    - (C) Archaic…. Sluggish
    - (D) Aged…. Expeditious

39. The chef was somewhat_____as he refused to use any ingredient that was not of a _____ quality and cost.
    - (A) Modest…. Highest
    - (B) Pretentious… Premium
    - (C) Ostentatious…. Common
    - (D) Inclusive…. Thwarted

40. A musician might _____some harmony from this chaos of noises, this _____ of sounds.
    - (A) Extract…. Jumble
    - (B) Find…. Repetition
    - (C) Disdain…. Pattern
    - (D) Hear…. Studio

Practice Test 2 – Reading Comprehension

36 Questions – 35 Minutes

Questions 1– 6:

1   When first discovered by the Spanish,
2 Peru was a flourishing empire, including two
3 kingdoms, Peru and Quito, that extended over
4 nearly half of the widest part of South
5 America. It had been governed by a long
6 succession of Emperors, who were called the
7 Incas of Peru.
8   On the 14th of Nov. 1524, three Spanish
9 adventurers named Francisco Pizarro (who had
10 been a hog feeder in earlier life), Diego de
11 Almagro, and Hernando Luque, set sail from
12 Panama with hopes of reaching Peru.
13   At Tumbez, about three degrees south of
14 the equator, Pizarro and his companions
15 feasted their eyes on the wealth and grandeur
16 of the Peruvian Empire. This place was
17 distinguished for its splendid temples and for
18 one of the palaces of the Incas, the emperors of
19 the country. But what chiefly attracted their
20 attention was the show of gold and silver, not
21 only in the peoples' personal ornaments and in
22 the temples, but also in common vases and
23 utensils, which left Pizarro with no doubt that
24 the metals were widely abundant. After
25 sufficiently exploring the country, Pizarro
26 hurried back to Spain, where he gained support
27 for taking over Peru from King Charles V.
28   Encouraged by three small ships and 186
29 soldiers, Pizarro returned to Panama and then
30 on to the Bay of St. Matthew. He then
31 advanced by land as quickly as possible toward

32 Peru. When Pizarro landed in the Bay of St.
33 Matthew, a civil war was raging between
34 Atahualpa, the Emperor of Peru, and his
35 brother. This contest occupied so much of the
36 Peruvian's attention that they never once
37 checked the Spaniards' progress, and Pizarro
38 aimed to take advantage of this distraction.
39   He directed his march towards Caxamalia,
40 a small town twelve days from St. Michael,
41 where Atahualpa was camped with a
42 considerable army. Before he proceeded
43 farther, an officer dispatched by the Inca met
44 him with valuable presents, an offer of
45 alliance, and the promise of a friendly
46 reception at Caxamalia.
47   Pizarro deployed the usual Spanish
48 trickery and pretended to come as an
49 ambassador of King Charles to offer his aid in
50 fighting the Incan Emperor's enemies.
51   The Peruvians were wholly unable to
52 understand the Spaniard's objectives. They
53 were not sure whether they should consider
54 them as superior beings who had come to help
55 (as the Spaniards wished them to believe) or
56 whether they were sent as evil demons to
57 punish the Inca for their crimes (as the
58 greediness and cruelty of the Spaniards led
59 them to believe).
60   However, Pizarro's declaration of
61 promoting peace removed the emperor's fears
62 so much that he decided to grant a friendly
63 welcome which he would later regret.

1. The text in parenthesis in lines 8 and 9 serves to …

    (A) Cast doubt on Pizzaro's status as a political adventurer.
    (B) Highlight that hog feeders make the best adventurers.
    (C) Show that Pizzaro achieved great status in life.
    (D) Detail Pizzaro's wide range of talents and interests.

2. How did King Charles V respond to Pizarro?

    (A) He told Pizarro to leave the Incan Empire's wealth alone.
    (B) He told Pizarro to help develop the Incan Empire's education system.
    (C) He told Pizarro he could govern the Incan Empire and take its wealth for Spain.
    (D) He told Pizarro to befriend the Incan Emperor and govern together.

3. In line 48, the word "trickery" most clearly means

    (A) Deception
    (B) Prank
    (C) Magic
    (D) Joke

4. The passage best supports which of the following statements?

    (A) Pizzaro was able to defeat the Incan armies with dishonesty.
    (B) If Spain had not attacked, Emperor Atahualpa would have won the civil war.
    (C) Sibling rivalries were common among Incan royal families.
    (D) Panama became an independent kingdom, free from Spanish rule.

5. By referring to the Incan civil war as a "contest" and "distraction", it can be said that the author views it as…

    (A) Significant
    (B) Critical
    (C) Unfavorable
    (D) Unimportant

6. What best describes the organization of the passage?

    (A) Events occur in order of importance to the plot.
    (B) The personality of each character is studied in relation to the others.
    (C) Events occur chronologically.
    (D) The events are unrelated but narrated from the same point of view.

Questions 7 – 12:

1 The story of the buffalo's daily life and
2 habits should begin with the "running season."
3 This period stretches through the months of
4 August and September and is characterized by
5 excitement and activity throughout the entire
6 herd. Their behavior during this period is quite
7 opposite to their usual easy-going and even
8 lethargic nature, a noticeable feature of the
9 bison's character at all other times.

10 Before the "running season," buffalos grow
11 in the summer months. The young calves are
12 two to four months old. Through continued
13 feasting on new crops of buffalo grasses and
14 bunch grasses—possibly the most nutritious in
15 the world—every buffalo in the herd grows
16 round, fat, and vigorous. By then, their faded
17 and weathered mats of last year's hair have
18 fallen off and been replaced by a new coat of
19 dark gray and black. Besides the shortness of
20 their hair, the buffalo are in their prime in the
21 summer.

22 During the "running season," as it is called
23 by the plainsmen, the nature of the herd is
24 completely changed. Instead of being broken
25 up into several small groups that are spread
26 over a vast territory, the herd comes together in
27 a dense and confused mass of thousands, so
28 closely congregated as to actually blacken the
29 face of the land. As if by an irresistible instinct,
30 every straggler is drawn into the center and, for
31 miles on every side, the country can be found
32 entirely deserted of buffalo.

33 At this time, the herd becomes a bustling
34 heap of activity and excitement. As usual, in
35 these situations, the bulls spend half their time
36 chasing the cows and fight each other during
37 the other half. These fights, which are always
38 over a few seconds after the first collision, are
39 preceded by common threats and displays. The
40 bull lowers his head until his nose almost
41 touches the ground, he roars like a foghorn
42 until the earth trembles, then glares madly at
43 his adversary with half-white eyeballs, and
44 with his front paws he ups the dry earth into a
45 great cloud of dust high above his back. At
46 such times, the combined roaring of many
47 huge bulls unites and forms a great volume of
48 sound like distant thunder, which has often
49 been heard at a distance of 1 to 3 miles. I have
50 even been assured by old plainsmen that under
51 favorable atmospheric conditions such sounds
52 have been heard five miles away.

7. Which sentence best expresses the main idea of the passage?

(A) Even though buffalo bulls often fight, the fights are short and non-lethal.

(B) Buffalo calves usually have reached three to four months old by August or September.

(C) From August through September, buffalo undergo major behavioral changes.

(D) Buffalos are almost always independent, calm animals.

8. According to the text, why are the bulls fighting?

(A) Because of the dense population of energized buffalos

(B) To protect their calves

(C) To protect their vast territory from invaders

(D) To get the attention of the cows

9. With which statement would the author be most likely to agree?

(A) Old plainsmen can hear the bulls roaring because they have trained their ears to do so.

(B) Though the running season is impressive, buffalo are best viewed between April and May.

(C) Buffalos' coats of fur are far more beautiful after a long winter.

(D) Buffalos are interesting and remarkable animals worth studying.

10. As used in line 8, the word "lethargic" most nearly means…

(A) Spirited.
(B) Drab.
(C) Sluggish.
(D) Tiresome.

11. Why does the author state that the history of a buffalo's daily life should start with the "running season"?

(A) This is a time in which buffalos are in their most normal state.

(B) This is a time in which buffalos are highly active and thus interesting to study.

(C) Male buffalos fight during this time.

(D) Buffalos have grown fat from eating grass by this time.

12. By likening the bulls' roars to thunder and a foghorn, the author's tone can be described as…

(A) Condescending.
(B) Diplomatic.
(C) Fearful.
(D) Amazed.

Questions 13 – 18

1   Nicholas Poussin (1594-1665) could have
2 belonged to the seventeenth century
3 considering that he was born so late in the
4 century before. Poussin was born in Normandy
5 and began to draw and paint quite early. He
6 studied some in France and, when he was thirty
7 years old, he went to Rome, where his artistic
8 career began in earnest.

9   He was a student of Andrea Sacchi and
10 also received some instruction from
11 Domenichino, but he formed his style
12 principally by studying the works of the
13 ancients of the great Raphael. He was so
14 devoted to studying the habits and customs of
15 the Greeks that he almost became one of them
16 in the way he thought.

17   When he first went to Rome, Poussin was
18 destitute and fameless, but he worked hard,
19 began to become well-known among the upper
20 class, and started receiving orders for pictures.
21 Louis XIII heard of Poussin, and invited him to
22 Paris, where he gave him apartments in the
23 Tuileries. But the artist longed to return to
24 Rome and made a plea to go back for his wife.
25 Soon after he left for Rome, Louis XIII died,
26 and Poussin never returned to France.

27

28   Poussin was always busy, but he asked
29 for such moderate prices that he was never
30 rich. When a great man pitied the artist
31 because he had so few servants, Poussin
32 pitied him in return for having so many. His
33 portrait painted by himself is in the Louvre,
34 where there are also many of his mythological
35 pictures. His love for the classic manner
36 makes these subjects his best works. His
37 paintings are seen in many European galleries
38 and in the Americas as well.

39   Should you wish to view the greatest
40 of his works, *The Abduction of the Sabine*
41 *Woman* and *Et In Arcadia Ego* can be found
42 in the Louvre and *Blind Orion Searching for*
43 *the Rising Sun* can be seen in the
44 Metropolitan Museum of Art, New York City.

13. Andrea Sacchi and Domenichino are both most likely to have been…

(A) Philosophy teachers.
(B) Upper-class patrons.
(C) Master artists.
(D) Descendants of the great Raphael.

14. The main purpose of the fourth paragraph (lines 27 to 33) is to…

(A) Depict Poussin as a humble man driven by the love of his craft.
(B) Criticize Poussin's decision to not charge more for his works.
(C) Explain why Poussin never returned to France.
(D) Portray Poussin as a social advocate opposed to the keeping of servants.

15. Poussin most likely used his wife as a reason to leave Paris because…

(A) She was gravely ill with smallpox.
(B) Poussin was a Republican opposed to the idea of working for a King.
(C) Poussin had grown tired of painting and wished to retire.
(D) It would have been dishonorable to simply quit such a prestigious position.

16. The author's intention in writing this passage is to…

(A) Explain the history of several famous paintings found in the Louvre and Metropolitan Museum of Art.
(B) Introduce the reader to the life of a famous European painter.
(C) Give some insight into the type of art that Louis XIII enjoyed.
(D) Tell the cautionary tale of a failed creative who only achieved fame after his death.

17. Which of the following best describes the organization of the passage?

(A) An artistic term is defined and explained through examples.
(B) The highlights of the main character's life are stated with supporting details.
(C) Important pieces of Poussin's work are introduced with varying degrees of criticism.
(D) A story is told to give insight into a personality.

18. As used in line 17, the word "destitute" most nearly means…

(A) Destined.
(B) Manipulated.
(C) Poor.
(D) Infamous.

1   Jascha Heifetz is good-natured,
2   unassuming and he has broad interests in art
3   and life beyond his gifted violin mastery,
4   proof that his talent is genuine and inborn.
5   Without such interests, no artist can become
6   genuinely great. Yet, Jascha Heifetz, with his
7   wonderful record of accomplishments and
8   awards and still more triumphs to come, does
9   not believe in "all work and no play."
10   He laughed when I put forward the idea
11   that he worked many hours a day, perhaps as
12   many as six or eight. "No," he said, "I do not
13   think I could ever have made any progress if I
14   had practiced six hours a day. In the first
15   place I have never believed in practicing too
16   much—it is just as bad as practicing too little!
17   And then there are so many other things I like
18   to do. I am fond of reading, and I like sports:
19   tennis, golf, cycling, boating, swimming, etc.
20   Often, when I am supposed to be practicing
21   hard, I am out with my camera, taking
22   pictures; for I have become what is known as
23   a 'camera fiend.' And just now I have a new
24   car, which I have learned to drive, and which
25   takes up a good deal of my time. I have never
26   believed in grinding. In fact, I think that if one

27   has to work very hard to get a piece, it will
28   show in the playing. To interpret music
29   properly, it is necessary to eliminate technical
30   difficulty; the audience should not feel the
31   artist struggle with what are considered hard
32   passages of music. I hardly ever practice more
33   than three hours a day on average, and
34   besides, I keep my Sundays free, when I do
35   not play at all, and sometimes I make an extra
36   holiday. As for six or seven hours a day, I
37   would not have been able to stand it at all."
38   I implied that what Mr. Heifetz said
39   might shock thousands of young violinists for
40   whom he pointed out a moral: "Of course," he
41   said, "you must not take me too literally.
42   Please do not think because I do not enjoy
43   over-practicing that one can go without it. I'm
44   quite frank to say I could not do it myself. But
45   there is a happy medium. I suppose that when
46   I play in public, it looks easy, but before I
47   ever came on the concert stage, I worked very
48   hard. And I do yet—but always putting the
49   two things together, mental work and physical
50   work. And when I reach a certain point in my
51   practice, as with everything else, there must
52   be relaxation."

19. Details in this passage are explained through…

(A) A biography.
(B) An analysis of a violinist's art.
(C) A dialogue.
(D) A series of examples.

20. The author states that for talent to be genuine, one must…

(A) Dedicate themselves to one art form and master it.
(B) Spend hours every day honing a skill until it is perfect.
(C) Show interest in things beyond what you are gifted in.
(D) Perform effortlessly so that the audience cannot sense the musician's struggle.

21. Which of the following is material evidence of Jasha Heifetz's mastery of the violin?

(A) Heifetz only practices for three hours a day.
(B) Heifetz's long record of awards and achievements.
(C) Heifetz has a wide range of interests including sports and photography.
(D) Heifetz interprets music well by eliminating technical difficulty.

22. The word "moral," as used in line 40 mostly nearly means…

(A) A lesson.
(B) Ethical.
(C) Team spirit.
(D) Conscience.

23. In the passage, the first-person narrator is most likely…

(A) A family member of Heifetz.
(B) A fellow violinist hoping to find a secret technique.
(C) A reporter writing a profile on the violinist.
(D) A music aficionado who had the privilege of an afternoon with their performer of choice.

24. The passage implies that if an audience can hear the difficulty of a particular passage of music…

(A) The musician must have practiced between 5 and 6 hours that day.
(B) The musician did not practice the passage enough.
(C) The musician is untalented and should not be performing such difficult music.
(D) The audience will not enjoy the performance as much as if it were played seamlessly.

1   Our country's forests are home to
2 hundreds of millions of animals, for which the
3 forests provide food and shelter. If we had no
4 forests, many of these birds and animals
5 would soon disappear. The acorns and other
6 nuts that the squirrels live off are examples of
7 the sustenance that the forest provides for its
8 residents.
9   In the clear, cold streams, there are many
10 different kinds of fish. If the forests were
11 destroyed by cutting or by fire, many of the
12 brooks and rivers would either dry up or the
13 water would become so low that thousands of
14 fish would die.
15   The most abundant animals of the forests
16 are deer, elk, antelope, and moose. Partridge,
17 grouse, quail, wild turkeys, and other game
18 birds are plentiful in some areas. The best-
19 known of all the inhabitants of the woods are
20 the squirrels. The presence of these many
21 birds and animals greatly adds to the
22 attractiveness of the forest.
23   Predatory animals, such as wolves, bears,
24 mountain lions, coyotes, and bobcats also live
25 in the forest. They kill much livestock each
26 year in the mountain regions of the western
27 states, and they also prey on some species of
28 bird life. The federal government and some
29 state governments now employ professional
30 hunters to trap and shoot these marauders.
31 Each year the hunters kill thousands of
32 predatory animals, thus saving the farmers
33 and cattle and sheep owners many thousands
34 of dollars.
35   Sportsmen are so numerous, and hunting
36 is so popular, that areas that do not allow for
37 hunting have to be established in the forests
38 and parks. When establishing a game refuge,
39 it is necessary to pick out a large plot of land
40 that contains enough food for the animals that
41 will inhabit it in both the summer and winter
42 months There are more than 11,640,648 acres
43 of forest land in the government game
44 refuges. California has 22 game refuges in her
45 17 national forests. New Mexico has 19,
46 while Montana, Idaho, Colorado,
47 Washington, and Oregon also have set aside
48 areas of government forest land for that
49 purpose. Were it not for these refuges where
50 hunting is not permitted, some of our best-
51 known wild game and birds would soon
52 become extinct.
53

25. The main idea of this passage is that…

(A) Hunters and sportsmen provide an essential service for wildlife.
(B) If allowed to survive unbridled, predatory animals would drive forest wildlife to extinction.
(C) Forests serve a crucially important purpose for wildlife and must be protected.
(D) Wildlife greatly adds to the attractiveness of forests.

26. The purpose of paragraph 5 (lines 35 to 52) is to explain the importance of…

(A) Hunters.
(B) Refuges.
(C) Wild animals.
(D) Predatory animals.

27. Based on its use in line 7, "sustenance" most closely means…

(A) Material.
(B) Maintenance.
(C) Shelter.
(D) Food.

28. Paragraph 1 (lines 1 to 8) does which of the following?

(A) Explains why forest lands have been disappearing over the past few years
(B) Introduces the topic and argument of the passage
(C) Gives multiple examples of animals that benefit from living in forests
(D) Sets up a position supporting the need for hunting

29. When discussing forest wildlife, the author's tone can best be described as…

(A) Uninterested.
(B) Optimistic.
(C) Sympathetic.
(D) Critical.

30. The author of this passage would be most likely to agree with which of the following statements?

(A) Wildlife should be preserved by allocating land to game refuges.
(B) Farmers should be willing to sacrifice a portion of their crop for the benefit of wildlife.
(C) Hunters and sportsmen have been overly restricted by needless regulations.
(D) While the game birds are beautiful, moose, elk, and deer are far more impressive animals.

1   In Puerto Rico, hurricanes occasionally
2   occur between July and October and rain
3   comes in torrents in September and October.
4   These daily showers of the rainy season
5   usually come in the late afternoon, but the sky
6   clears up with the setting sun. The hurricanes
7   are sometimes accompanied by earthquake
8   shocks. People may be injured or killed, and
9   their homes destroyed during these violent
10 storms. Puerto Rico, however, is freer from
11 them than other islands in the West Indies.
12   It is easy to tell when a hurricane is
13 approaching. The wind dies away, and a
14 deathly stillness falls over everything. There
15 is not even a slight breeze. The leaves droop
16 on the trees and the heat becomes oppressive.
17 The sky becomes copper-colored and tints
18 everything with a ghastly hue. The cattle and
19 other animals seem to know that danger is
20 near and run around in a terrified way.
21   Far out in the ocean, the water is calm
22 and smooth; but near the shore, the waves
23 rush angrily onto the beach with a mighty
24 roar. By and by the wind begins to rise, just a
25 little; first from one direction, and then from
26 another. This is a sign that the storm is

27 nearby. Very soon a fearful roar can be heard
28 and, all at once, the hurricane descends on the
29 island. The destruction begins. Trees are
30 uprooted, growing crops are laid to waste, and
31 houses are torn down and scattered in every
32 direction. Sometimes whole villages are
33 destroyed, and many people are killed or
34 wounded.
35   When the barometer warns of an
36 approaching storm, people prepare for it.
37 They hunt for shelter and take with them a
38 supply of cane juice and food to last until the
39 storm subsides. People defend as much as
40 possible from hurricanes by building their
41 houses of stone with massive walls. They
42 provide strong bars for doors and windows.
43 Doors and window shutters are closed, barred,
44 and double locked, and the town looks as if it
45 were deserted by all human beings.
46   Add to this the howling of the blasts and
47 the crash of falling trees and one can picture
48 the terrible scene. To venture out is almost
49 certain death because the air is so full of
50 flying missiles of boards, bricks, tiles, stones,
51 and branches of trees.

31. The passage implies that, when a hurricane comes ashore, the people of Puerto Rico…

(A) Have prepared by taking the cows to shelter.
(B) Are prepared with ample supplies of cane juice and food for their families.
(C) Know there is little they can do to prepare.
(D) Have nothing to worry about from the storm.

32. The author states that Puerto Rico is freer from hurricanes than other islands in the West Indies to…

(A) Assure the reader that Puerto Rico's weather is not as dangerous as the passage may suggest.
(B) Sway the reader into a false sense of hope for the population of Puerto Rico.
(C) Introduce the next topic, Jamaica, another island in the West Indies.
(D) Provide context for the reader by showing the severity of seasonal weather in the region.

33. Based on its use in line 16, the word "oppressive" most closely means…

(A) Tyrannical.
(B) Bigoted.
(C) Domineering.
(D) Suffocating.

34. This passage would most likely be found in which of the following print sources?

(A) An encyclopedia of Latin American cultures
(B) A tourism brochure
(C) A climate overview of Caribbean islands
(D) An engineering dossier for future builders

35. Puerto Rico's hurricane season occurs during which of the following months?

(A) April through May
(B) June through July
(C) July through October
(D) October through December

36. What best describes the author's tone when describing hurricanes?
(A) Critical
(B) Cautionary
(C) Optimistic
(D) Indifferent

Practice Test 2 – Essay

Essay Topic:

Should schools ban cell phones? Why or why not?

Write your essay in the space below:

_____

_____

_____

_____

_____

_____

_____

_____

_____

_____

_____

_____

_____

_____

_____

_____

_____

_____

_____

Practice Test 2 – Verbal Reasoning Answers

1. B	15. C	29. C
2. A	16. A	30. D
3. B	17. B	31. A
4. B	18. C	32. B
5. A	19. A	33. D
6. A	20. C	34. A
7. C	21. A	35. B
8. A	22. B	36. A
9. C	23. A	37. A
10. B	24. D	38. C
11. A	25. C	39. B
12. C	26. A	40. A
13. B	27. B	
14. C	28. D	

Practice Test 2 – Reading Comprehension Answers

1. A	13. C	25. C
2. C	14. A	26. B
3. A	15. D	27. D
4. A	16. B	28. B
5. D	17. B	29. C
6. C	18. C	30. A
7. C	19. C	31. B
8. A	20. A	32. D
9. D	21. B	33. D
10. C	22. A	34. C
11. B	23. C	35. C
12. D	24. D	36. B

Practice Test 2 – Reading Comprehension –
Where to Find the Answers

Passage 1:

1. **A - Cast doubt on Pizzaro's status as a political adventurer.**

8   On the 14th of Nov. 1524, three Spanish
9   adventurers named Francisco Pizarro (who had
10   been a hog feeder in earlier life), Diego de
11   Almagro, and Hernando Luque, set sail from
12   Panama with hopes of reaching Peru.

2. **C - He told Pizarro he could govern the Incan Empire and take its wealth for Spain.**

24   the metals were widely abundant. After
25   sufficiently exploring the country, Pizarro
26   hurried back to Spain, where he gained support
27   for taking over Peru from King Charles V.

3. **A - Deception**

47   Pizarro deployed the usual Spanish
48   trickery and pretended to come as an
49   ambassador of King Charles to offer his aid in
50   fighting the Incan Emperor's enemies.

4. **A - Pizzaro was able to defeat the Incan armies with dishonesty.**

60   However, Pizarro's declaration of
61   promoting peace removed the emperor's fears
62   so much that he decided to grant a friendly
63   welcome which he would later regret.

5. **D - Unimportant**

33   Matthew, a civil war was raging between
34   Atahualpa, the Emperor of Peru, and his
35   brother. This contest occupied so much of the
36   Peruvian's attention that they never once
37   checked the Spaniards' progress, and Pizarro
38   aimed to take advantage of this distraction.

6. **C – Events occur chronologically.**

1   When first discovered by the Spanish, Peru
2   was a flourishing empire, including two

8   On the 14th of Nov. 1524, three Spanish

28   Encouraged by three small ships and 186
29   soldiers, Pizarro returned to Panama and then
30   on to the Bay of St. Matthew. He then
31   advanced by land as quickly as possible toward

Passage 2:

7. **C - From August through September, buffalo undergo major behavioral changes.**

1   The story of the buffalo's daily life and habits
2   should begin with the "running season." This
3   period stretches through the months of August
4   and September and is characterized by
5   excitement and activity throughout the entire
6   herd. Their behavior during this period is quite
7   opposite to their usual easy-going and even
8   lethargic nature, a noticeable feature of the
9   bison's character at all other times.

8. **A - Because of the dense population of energized buffalos**

22   During the "running season," as it is called
23   by the plainsmen, the nature of the herd is
24   completely changed. Instead of being broken
25   up into several small groups that are spread
26   over a vast territory, the herd comes together in

27   a dense and confused mass of thousands, so
28   closely congregated as to actually blacken the
29   face of the land. As if by an irresistible instinct,
30   every straggler is drawn into the center and, for
31   miles on every side, the country can be found
32   entirely deserted of buffalo.
33   At this time, the herd becomes a bustling
34   heap of activity and excitement. As usual, in
35   these situations, the bulls spend half their time
36   chasing the cows and fight each other during
37   the other half. These fights, which are always

9. **D - Buffalos are interesting and remarkable animals worth studying.**

If the author writes a whole passage on the topic, they most likely think it is interesting and worth studying! You could also use process of elimination here.

10. **C – Sluggish.**

5   excitement and activity throughout the entire
6   herd. Their behavior during this period is quite
7   opposite to their usual easy-going and even
8   lethargic nature, a noticeable feature of the
9   bison's character at all other times.

11. **B - This is a time in which buffalos are highly active and thus interesting to study.**

1   The story of the buffalo's daily life and habits
2   should begin with the "running season." This
3   period stretches through the months of August
4   and September and is characterized by
5   excitement and activity throughout the entire
6   herd. Their behavior during this period is quite
7   opposite to their usual easy-going and even
8   lethargic nature, a noticeable feature of the
9   bison's character at all other times.

12. **D – Amazed**

40   bull lowers his head until his nose almost
41   touches the ground, he roars like a foghorn
42   until the earth trembles, then glares madly at
43   his adversary with half-white eyeballs, and
44   with his front paws he ups the dry earth into a
45   great cloud of dust high above his back. At
46   such times, the combined roaring of many
47   huge bulls unites and forms a great volume of
48   sound like distant thunder, which has often
49   been heard at a distance of 1 to 3 miles. I have
50   even been assured by old plainsmen that under
51   favorable atmospheric conditions such sounds
52   have been heard five miles away.

Passage 3:

13. C - Master Artists.

4   century before. Poussin was born in Normandy
5   and began to draw and paint quite early. He
6   studied some in France and, when he was thirty
7   years old, he went to Rome, where his artistic
8   career began in earnest.
9   He was a student of Andrea Sacchi and
10   also received some instruction from
11   Domenichino, but he formed his style
12   principally by studying the works of the
13   ancients of the great Raphael. He was so
14   devoted to studying the habits and customs of
15   the Greeks that he almost became one of them
16   in the way he thought.

14. A- Depict Poussin as a humble man driven by the love of his craft.

28   Poussin was always busy, but he asked
29   for such moderate prices that he was never
30   rich. When a great man pitied the artist
31   because he had so few servants, Poussin
32   pitied him in return for having so many. His
33   portrait painted by himself is in the Louvre,
34   where there are also many of his mythological
35   pictures. His love for the classic manner
36   makes these subjects his best works. His
37   paintings are seen in many European galleries
38   and in the Americas as well.

15. D - It would have been dishonorable to simply quit such a prestigious position.

23   Tuileries. But the artist longed to return to
24   Rome and made a plea to go back for his wife.
25   Soon after he left for Rome, Louis XIII died,
26   and Poussin never returned to France.

16. B - Introduce the reader to the life of a famous European painter.

1   Nicholas Poussin (1594-1665) could have
2   belonged to the seventeenth century
3   considering that he was born so late in the
4   century before. Poussin was born in Normandy
5   and began to draw and paint quite early. He

36   makes these subjects his best works. His
37   paintings are seen in many European galleries
38   and in the Americas as well.
39   Should you wish to view the greatest
40   of his works, *The Abduction of the Sabine*
41   *Woman* and *Et In Arcadia Ego* can be found
42   in the Louvre and *Blind Orion Searching for*
43   *the Rising Sun* can be seen in the
44   Metropolitan Museum of Art, New York City.

17. B - The highlights of the main character's life are stated with supporting details.

1   Nicholas Poussin (1594-1665) could have
2   belonged to the seventeenth century
3   considering that he was born so late in the
4   century before. Poussin was born in Normandy

9   He was a student of Andrea Sacchi and
10   also received some instruction from
11   Domenichino, but he formed his style

17   When he first went to Rome, Poussin was
18   destitute and fameless, but he worked hard,
19   began to become well-known among the upper

18. C – Poor.

17   When he first went to Rome, Poussin was
18   destitute and fameless, but he worked hard,
19   began to become well-known among the upper

165

Passage 4:

19. C – A dialogue.

10   He laughed when I put forward the idea
11   that he worked many hours a day, perhaps as
12   many as six or eight. "No," he said, "I do not
13   think I could ever have made any progress if I

38   I implied that what Mr. Heifetz said
39   might shock thousands of young violinists for
40   whom he pointed out a moral: "Of course," he

20. A - Dedicate themselves to one art form and master it.

45   there is a happy medium. I suppose that when
46   I play in public, it looks easy, but before I
47   ever came on the concert stage, I worked very
48   hard. And I do yet—but always putting the
49   two things together, mental work and physical
50   work. And when I reach a certain point in my
51   practice, as with everything else, there must
52   be relaxation."

21. B - Heifetz's long record of awards and achievements.

6   genuinely great. Yet, Jascha Heifetz, with his
7   wonderful record of accomplishments and
8   awards and still more triumphs to come, does
9   not believe in "all work and no play."

22. A – A lesson.

40   whom he pointed out a moral: "Of course," he
41   said, "you must not take me too literally.
42   Please do not think because I do not enjoy
43   over-practicing that one can go without it. I'm
44   quite frank to say I could not do it myself. But
45   there is a happy medium. I suppose that when

23. C - A reporter writing a profile on the violinist.

10   He laughed when I put forward the idea
11   that he worked many hours a day, perhaps as
12   many as six or eight. "No," he said, "I do not
13   think I could ever have made any progress if I

38   I implied that what Mr. Heifetz said
39   might shock thousands of young violinists for
40   whom he pointed out a moral: "Of course," he

24. D - The audience will not enjoy the performance as much as if it were played seamlessly.

27   has to work very hard to get a piece, it will
28   show in the playing. To interpret music
29   properly, it is necessary to eliminate technical
30   difficulty; the audience should not feel the
31   artist struggle with what are considered hard
32   passages of music. I hardly ever practice more

Passage 5:

25. C - Forests serve a crucially important purpose for wildlife and must be protected.

1   Our country's forests are home to hundreds
2 of millions of animals, for which the forests
3 provide food and shelter. If we had no forests,
4 many of these birds and animals would soon
5 disappear. The acorns and other nuts that the

26. B – Refuges.

49 purpose. Were it not for these refuges where
50 hunting is not permitted, some of our best-
51 known wild game and birds would soon
52 become extinct.

27. D - Food

5 would soon disappear. The acorns and other
6 nuts that the squirrels live off are examples of
7 the sustenance that the forest provides for its
8 residents.

28. B – Introduces the topic and argument of the passage

1   Our country's forests are home to hundreds
2 of millions of animals, for which the forests
3 provide food and shelter. If we had no forests,
4 many of these birds and animals would soon
5 disappear. The acorns and other nuts that the
6 squirrels live off are examples of the
7 sustenance that the forest provides for its
8 residents.

29. C – Sympathetic.

9   In the clear, cold streams, there are many
10 different kinds of fish. If the forests were
11 destroyed by cutting or by fire, many of the
12 brooks and rivers would either dry up or the
13 water would become so low that thousands of
14 fish would die.

30. A - Wildlife should be preserved by allocating land to game refuges.

49 purpose. Were it not for these refuges where
50 hunting is not permitted, some of our best-
51 known wild game and birds would soon
52 become extinct.

Passage 6:

31. **B - Are prepared with ample supplies of cane juice and food for their families.**

35   When the barometer warns of an
36   approaching storm, people prepare for it.
37   They hunt for shelter and take with them a
38   supply of cane juice and food to last until the
39   storm subsides. People defend as much as

32. **D - Provide context for the reader by showing the severity of seasonal weather in the region.**

7   are sometimes accompanied by earthquake
8   shocks. People may be injured or killed, and
9   their homes destroyed during these violent
10   storms. Puerto Rico, however, is freer from
11   them than other islands in the West Indies.

33. **D – Suffocating.**

13   approaching. The wind dies away, and a
14   deathly stillness falls over everything. There is
15   not even a slight breeze. The leaves droop on
16   the trees and the heat becomes oppressive. The
17   sky becomes copper-colored and tints

34. **C - A climate overview of Caribbean islands**

1   In Puerto Rico, hurricanes occasionally
2   occur between July and October and rain
3   comes in torrents in September and October.
4   These daily showers of the rainy season
5   usually come in the late afternoon, but the sky
6   clears up with the setting sun. The hurricanes

35. **C – July through October**

1   In Puerto Rico, hurricanes occasionally
2   occur between July and October and rain
3   comes in torrents in September and October.

36. **B - Cautionary**

48   the terrible scene. To venture out is almost
49   certain death because the air is so full of
50   flying missiles of boards, bricks, tiles, stones,
51   and branches of trees.

Practice Test 2 – Essay Checklist

Introduction:

☐ The introduction paragraph is two to three sentences.

☐ The introduction paragraph ends with a thesis statement.

☐ The thesis statement responds to the questions and includes key reasons.

Body Paragraphs:

☐ The essay has two or three body paragraphs (three for upper level).

☐ Each body paragraph starts with a topic sentence.

☐ Each body paragraph has specific evidence.

Conclusion:

☐ The conclusion paragraph is two to three sentences.

☐ The conclusion paragraph starts with a restated thesis statement.

Overall Writing Quality:

☐ Each paragraph is indented.

☐ Writing is clear.

☐ Word choice is formal.

☐ The essay fully responds to the prompt.

☐ The essay shows positive qualities about the student. (Remember, the schools are reading it, and it is not given a score.)

Scoring Practice Test 2

Use this chart to approximate your percentile score based on your number of correct answers. The actual scoring is scaled based on the difficulty of the test you receive, so this is just an approximate score.

Middle Level

	# of Correct Answers	# of Correct Answers	# of Correct Answers
7th Grade Verbal Reasoning	20	26	31
7th Grade Reading Comprehension	19	25	31
8th Grade Verbal Reasoning	21	27	33
8th Grade Reading Comprehension	20	26	31
Percentile	25th	50th	75th

Upper Level

	# of Correct Answers	# of Correct Answers	# of Correct Answers
9th Grade Verbal Reasoning	22	28	34
9th Grade Reading Comprehension	21	27	32
10th Grade Verbal Reasoning	23	29	35
10th Grade Reading Comprehension	22	29	33
11th and 12th Grade Verbal Reasoning	25	31	36
11th and 12th Grade Reading Comprehension	24	30	34
Percentile	25th	50th	75th

Practice Test # 3

Practice Test 3 – Verbal Reasoning

40 Questions – 20 Minutes

Part One—Synonyms

Directions: Select the word that is most nearly the same in meaning as the word in capital letters.

1. FLATTER
    - (A) Determine
    - (B) Praise
    - (C) Imagine
    - (D) Trust

2. REPRIMAND
    - (A) Scold
    - (B) Tame
    - (C) Encourage
    - (D) Exhaust

3. FICKLE
    - (A) Unpredictable
    - (B) Hostile
    - (C) Playful
    - (D) Generous

4. ACCOMMODATE
    - (A) Interrupt
    - (B) Adapt
    - (C) Applaud
    - (D) Pity

5. ALLEVIATE
    - (A) Ease
    - (B) Depress
    - (C) Harden
    - (D) Grow

6. GREGARIOUS
    - (A) Calm
    - (B) Reliable
    - (C) Social
    - (D) Annoying

7. FLOURISH
    - (A) diminish
    - (B) prosper
    - (C) simplify
    - (D) vanish

8. KINETIC

   (A) Dynamic

   (B) Inert

   (C) Potential

   (D) Static

9. INNATE

   (A) Acquired

   (B) Inherent

   (C) Learned

   (D) Unnatural

10. JUBILANT

   (A) Depressed

   (B) Joyful

   (C) Relaxed

   (D) Wary

11. ABATE

   (A) Diminish

   (B) Enhance

   (C) Intensify

   (D) Prolong

12. AMBIGUOUS

   (A) clear

   (B) definite

   (C) equivocal

   (D) straightforward

13. EPHEMERAL

   (A) Enduring

   (B) Fleeting

   (C) Permanent

   (D) Timeless

14. LUCID

   (A) Confusing

   (B) Obscure

   (C) Transparent

   (D) Vague

15. OBSTINATE

   (A) Resolute

   (B) Flaw

   (C) Ideal

   (D) Mistake

16. INSOLENT

   (A) Unfortunate

   (B) Rude

   (C) Congenial

   (D) Keen

17. BENIGN

   (A) Beneficial

   (B) Malignant

   (C) Worrisome

   (D) Toxic

18. CANDOR

   (A) Deceit

   (B) Frankness

   (C) Reserve

   (D) Silence

19. LETHARGIC

   (A) Energetic

   (B) Lazy

   (C) Lively

   (D) Vigorous

20. HAPHAZARD

   (A) Organized

   (B) Random

   (C) Regular

   (D) Systematic

Part Two—Sentence Completion

Directions: Select the word or word pair that best completes the sentence.

21. The novelist's new book, which offers a deeply moving narrative of personal loss and redemption, has been _____ by critics and readers alike.
    (A) denounced
    (B) besieged
    (C) lauded
    (D) trivialized

22. The scientist's theory, initially met with _____, has now become the foundation of modern physics.
    (A) approval
    (B) indifference
    (C) ridicule
    (D) support

23. Due to the _____ nature of her illness, she was often unable to predict when she would feel well.
    (A) consistent
    (B) erratic
    (C) mild
    (D) stable

24. Despite his _____ personality, he was surprisingly well-liked among his colleagues.
    (A) amiable
    (B) antagonistic
    (C) benign
    (D) gregarious

25. The company's _____ approach to marketing and diversion from the old ways has significantly increased its customer base.
    (A) innovative
    (B) predictable
    (C) rudimentary
    (D) traditional

26. The _____ of the proposal ensured that it was easily understood by all of the board members.
    (A) ambiguity
    (B) clarity
    (C) obscurity
    (D) vagueness

27. During the early 20th century, many scientists believed that Mars was _____; later discoveries revealed the planet to be barren and inhospitable.
    (A) desolate
    (B) empty
    (C) fertile
    (D) lifeless

28. The detective's _____ attention to detail led to the resolution of the complex case.
    - (A) casual
    - (B) meticulous
    - (C) negligent
    - (D) superficial

29. Despite the challenges, the team _____ and completed the project ahead of schedule.
    - (A) faltered
    - (B) failed
    - (C) persevered
    - (D) wavered

30. The documentary showed a true picture and provided a _____ view of the daily struggles faced by the community.
    - (A) biased
    - (B) candid
    - (C) distorted
    - (D) superficial

31. Poaching, overhunting, and severe habitat loss have led to the catastrophic _____ of the tiger population, resulting in only 3,900 tigers left in the wild.
    - (A) Inflation
    - (B) Reduction
    - (C) Deafening
    - (D) Pinnacle

32. The smallpox vaccine, which was developed by Edward Jenner in 1796, was the first successful vaccine to be produced and was ultimately able to _____ many people.
    - (A) Threaten
    - (B) Assure
    - (C) Safeguard
    - (D) Supplement

33. With the meal still being prepared, the children arguing, and the guests arriving rapidly, the family holiday was sure to be a _____ one.
    - (A) Chaotic
    - (B) Sincere
    - (C) Bashful
    - (D) Serene

34. Although she needed the income, she decided to _____ the job at the clothing store because she had received reports of inhumane conditions in their factories, and she did not want to support the company.
    - (A) Accept
    - (B) Withstand
    - (C) Forfeit
    - (D) Supply

35. The athlete's performance was _____ by his injury, but his determination to win never _____

    (A) enhanced . . . waned
    (B) hindered . . . faltered
    (C) improved . . . wavered
    (D) unaffected . . . ceased

36. While there were other contributing factors, the formation of the alliances was ultimately the _____ cause of WWI, because the conflict between the central powers and the allied powers drove the countries into war.

    (A) Secondary
    (B) Principal
    (C) Detrimental
    (D) Temporary

37. Despite the company's claims of being environmentally friendly, their practices _____ the local ecosystem and _____ the trust of the community.

    (A) protected . . . gained
    (B) harmed . . . eroded
    (C) preserved . . . built
    (D) revitalized . . . undermined

38. Although the new policy was designed to _____ the workforce, it inadvertently _____ overall productivity.

    (A) benefit . . . decreased
    (B) motivate . . .saturated
    (C) streamline . . . increased
    (D) support . . . boosted

39. The novel's protagonist was _____ in his pursuits and his decisions often led to _____ consequences.

    (A) diligent . . . favorable
    (B) reckless . . . disastrous
    (C) steadfast . . . trivial
    (D) uncertain . . . positive

40. The teacher's methods were both _____ and _____, encouraging students to think critically while adhering to a structured curriculum.

    (A) rigid . . . flexible
    (B) innovative . . . traditional
    (C) monotonous . . . engaging
    (D) lenient . . . strict

Practice Test 3 – Reading Comprehension

36 Questions – 35 Minutes

<u>Questions 1-6:</u>

1   The function of water in nature is
2 essentially that of a solvent or a medium of
3 circulation; it is not, in any sense, food, yet
4 without it, no food can be taken in by an
5 animal. Without water the solid materials of
6 the globe would be unable to come together so
7 closely as to interchange their elements, and
8 there would be no circulation of matter to
9 speak of, and the earth would be, as it were,
10 locked up or dead.
11   When we look upon water as the
12 nearest approach to a universal solvent that
13 even the astute scientist of today has been able
14 to discover, it is clear why it can never be
15 found in an absolutely pure form in nature. For
16 wherever it accumulates it dissolves something
17 from its surroundings. Still, in a raindrop just
18 formed, we have very nearly pure water, but
19 even this contains dissolved air to the extent of
20 about one-fiftieth of its volume, and as the drop
21 falls downward it takes up such impurities as
22 may be floating in the atmosphere. For
23 example, if our raindrop is falling immediately
24 after a long drought, it becomes charged with
25 nitrate or nitrite of ammonia and various
26 organic matters—perhaps also the spores or

27 germs of disease. Thus, it will be seen that rain
28 tends to wonderfully clear or wash the
29 atmosphere, and we all know how much a first
30 rain is appreciated as an air purifier, and how it
31 carries down with its valuable food for plants.
32   The rainwater, in percolating through or over
33 the land, flows mainly toward the rivers, and in
34 doing so it becomes charged with mineral
35 matter, lime salts, and common salt. Some of
36 that water which has penetrated more deeply
37 into the earth takes up far more solid matter
38 than is ordinarily found in river water. The
39 bulk of this impure water tends toward the
40 ocean, taking with it its load of salt and lime.
41   Constant evaporation, of course, takes
42 place from the surface of the sea, so that the
43 salt and lime accumulate, this latter being,
44 however, ultimately deposited as shells, coral,
45 and chalk, while nearly pure or naturally
46 distilled water once more condenses in the
47 form of clouds. This process, by which a
48 constant supply of purified water is kept up in
49 the natural economy, is imitated on a small
50 scale when water is converted into steam by
51 the action of heat, and this vapor is cooled to
52 reproduce liquid water, which is known as the
53 process of distillation.

1. Which sentence best expresses the main idea of the passage?
   (A) Rain cleans the air.
   (B) Water is a solvent that can be purified by distillation.
   (C) River water flows toward the ocean filled with impurities.
   (D) Water from the ocean evaporates to form clouds.

2. The primary purpose of the fourth paragraph (lines 40-52) is to…
   (A) Tell how shells are formed.
   (B) Give a warning about how much salt and lime are in ocean water.
   (C) Show that river water is not clean.
   (D) Explain how water can be purified and distilled.

3. In line 2, the word "medium" most closely means…
   (A) Sorcerer.
   (B) Halfway point.
   (C) Way or means
   (D) Mid-size.

4. With which statement about water distillation would the author most likely agree?

   (A) Distillation is the way to purify water.
   (B) Collecting water in nature is the best way to tell if water is absolutely pure.
   (C) We do not yet know how to distill water.
   (D) A water filter will remove all impurities from river water.

5. The passage implies that water found in nature can never be pure because…

   (A) It is regularly changing forms.
   (B) It is constantly accumulating other matter from its surroundings.
   (C) It is impossible to purify.
   (D) It is unable to reach a high enough temperature.

6. When using the word *dead* in line 9, the author's tone can best be described as…

   (A) Silly.
   (B) Serious.
   (C) Threatening.
   (D) Cheerful.

Questions 7-12:

Once an untamed colt is separated from the herd, the next step will be to get the horse into a stable or shed. This should be done as quietly as possible, so as not to excite any suspicion in the horse of any danger befalling him. The best way to do this is to lead a tame and gentle horse into the stable first and hitch him, then quietly walk around the untamed colt, and let him go in of his own accord. It is almost impossible to get helpers, who have never practiced on this principle, to go slow and considerately enough about it. In handling a wild horse, above all other things, that good old saying is true, "haste makes waste;" that is, waste of time and effort.

One wrong move may frighten your horse and make him think it is necessary to escape despite all hazards for the safety of his life, and thus make two hours work of a ten-minute job. This would be all your own fault, and entirely unnecessary; for he will not run unless you run after him, and that would not be a good plan unless you knew that you could outrun him; or you will have to let him stop of his own accord after all. But he will not try to break away unless you attempt to force him into measures.

If he does not see the way at once and is a little fretful about going in, do not undertake to drive him, but give him a little less room outside, by gently closing in around him. Do not raise your arms but let them hang at your side; for you might as well raise a club. If he attempts to turn back, walk before him, but do not run; and if he gets past you, encircle him again in the same quiet manner, and he will soon find that you are not going to hurt him, and you can soon walk so close around him that he will go into the stable for more room, and to get farther from you.

As soon as he is in, remove the gentle and tame horse that you used as a helper, and shut the door. This will be his first notion of confinement—not knowing how to get in such a place, nor how to get out of it. That he may take it as quietly as possible, see that the shed is entirely free from dogs, chickens, or anything that would annoy him; then give him a few ears of corn, and let him remain alone fifteen or twenty minutes, until he has examined his apartment, and has become reconciled to this new environment. At this point, the colt has relaxed, and you will begin planning how to put a halter on him.

7. Which sentence best expresses the main idea of the passage?
   (A) Wild horses will not go into a stable easily.
   (B) You need to show an untamed colt who is the boss.
   (C) Getting an untamed colt into a stable is best done calmly and quietly.
   (D) A tamed, gentle horse can help you coax an untamed colt into a stable.

8. The primary purpose of the second paragraph (lines 16-27) is to…

   (A) List hazards and the need for safety around horses.
   (B) Explain the importance and practicality of not doing anything that would frighten the untamed colt.
   (C) Tell a story about chasing a horse.
   (D) Show the impossibility of taming wild colts because one wrong move will frighten them.

9. In line 25, the word "accord" most closely means…

   (A) Treaty.
   (B) Musical notes.
   (C) Rope.
   (D) Will.

10. With which statement about stabling untamed colts would the author most likely agree?

    (A) Gentleness and patience are the keys to success.
    (B) You need to wave your arms to herd a wild colt in the right direction.
    (C) Smart horse trainers are forceful and loud.
    (D) Putting tamed horses with wild ones will only cause the tame ones to become wilder.

11. The fourth sentence of the first paragraph (lines 9-15) implies that most people…

    (A) Are capable of helping to herd an untamed colt.
    (B) Like to help herd young colts.
    (C) Are not patient and focused enough to help herd an untamed colt.
    (D) Know how to be calm and quiet enough to keep from startling an untamed colt.

12. The author's tone can best be described as…

    (A) Cautionary.
    (B) Humorous.
    (C) Disinterested.
    (D) Admiring.

Not only do comets present great varieties in appearance, but even the shape and size of a single comet undergoes great change. The comet will sometimes increase enormously in bulk; sometimes it will diminish; sometimes it will have a large tail, or sometimes no tail at all. Measurements of a comet's size are almost futile; they may cease to be true even during the few hours in which a comet is observed over one night. It is, in fact, impossible to identify a comet by any description of its individual appearance. Yet the question as to the identity of a comet is often of very great consequence. We must provide means by which it can be established, entirely apart from what the comet may look like.

Often, the head of a comet, containing its brightest spot, is called the nucleus, and in this part, the material of the comet seems to be much denser than elsewhere. Surrounding the nucleus, we find certain definite layers of luminous material, the coma, or head, from 20,000 to 1,000,000 miles in diameter, from which the tail seems to stream away.

This view may be regarded as that of a typical object of this class, but the varieties of structure presented by different comets are almost innumerable. In some cases, we find the nucleus absent; in other cases, we find the tail to be wanting. The tail is, no doubt, a conspicuous feature in those great comets that receive universal attention; but in the small telescopic objects, of which a few are generally found every year, this feature is usually absent.

It is now well known that several of these comets make periodic returns. After having been invisible for a certain number of years, a comet comes into view and again retreats into space to perform another revolution. The question then arises as to how we are to recognize the body when it does come back. The specific features of its size or brightness, the presence or absence of a tail, large or small, are fleeting characters of no value for such a purpose.

Newton devised a method by which, from the known facts, the path which the comet pursues could be determined. He found that it was a parabola, and that the velocity of the comet was governed by the law that the straight line from the sun to the comet swept over equal areas in equal times. Thus, individual comets can be identified and tracked by their path.

13. Which sentence best expresses the main idea of the paragraph...
    (A) Comets all have the same shape but follow different parabolic paths.
    (B) Comets are always easily visible and have the same shape as a comma.
    (C) Comets follow a different path on each revolution.
    (D) Each comet changes often in appearance, therefore, we must determine its repetitive path to identify it as a particular comet.

14. The primary purpose of the second paragraph (lines 18-28) is to...

    (A) Provide details of the tail of the comet
    (B) Explain how comets frequently change in shape, size, and structure.
    (C) Explain the structure of a comet.
    (D) Show that each comet stays in the same basic shape even if its size changes.

15. In line 37, the word "periodic" most closely means...

    (A) Random.
    (B) Conclusive.
    (C) Occasional.
    (D) Large.

16. With which statement about comets would the author most likely agree?

    (A) Comets are beautiful but dangerous.
    (B) Tracking a comet's changes in appearance is important work.
    (C) A comet can be identified by the path of its revolution.
    (D) There is always a nucleus at the head of a comet.

17. The passage implies that...

    (A) There are so many comets that no one can keep track of them.
    (B) It is impossible to identify a comet just by how it looks.
    (C) Most people can define the characteristics of a comet.
    (D) Comets are fun to watch.

18. Which statement best describes the organization of the passage?

    (A) A phenomenon is introduced and then explained in detail.
    (B) A series of events are explained chronologically.
    (C) A series of terms are defined and detailed.
    (D) A theory is proposed and then refuted.

Questions 19 – 24:

A story was told by Lincoln himself to a few friends one evening in the Executive Mansion in Washington. The President said: "You never heard, did you, how I earned my first dollar? We had succeeded in raising, chiefly by my labor, sufficient produce to take down the river to sell. After much persuasion, I got the consent of my mother to go and constructed a little flatboat, large enough to take a barrel or two of things that we had gathered, with myself and the bundle, down to the Southern market.

A steamer was coming down the river. The custom was, if passengers were at any of the landings, for them to go out in a boat and wait for the steamer to stop and take them on board. I was contemplating my new flatboat and wondering whether I could make it stronger or improve it in any way, when two men came down to the shore in carriages with trunks. Looking at the different boats, they singled out mine and asked, 'Who owns this?' I answered somewhat modestly, 'I do.' 'Will you take us and our trunks to the steamer?' asked one of them. 'Certainly,' said I. I was glad to have the chance of earning something. I supposed that each of them would give me two or three bits.

The trunks were put on my flatboat, the passengers seated themselves on the trunks, and I rowed them out to the steamer. They got on board, and I lifted up their heavy trunks and put them on the deck. The steamer was about to put on steam again, when I called out to them that they had forgotten to pay me. Each man took from his pocket a silver half-dollar and threw it into the bottom of my boat.

I could scarcely believe my eyes. Gentlemen, you may think it a little thing, and in these days, it seems to me a trifle; but it was a great event in my life. I could scarcely believe that I, a poor boy, had earned a dollar in less than a day, —that by honest work I had earned a dollar. The world seemed wider and more beautiful to me. I was a more hopeful and confident being from that time."

19. Which sentence best expresses the main idea of the passage?
    (A) It is easy to earn a dollar.
    (B) Rowing a boat is a good way to earn money.
    (C) Lincoln fondly remembers the first time he earned a dollar.
    (D) Lincoln liked to tell stories.

20. The primary purpose of the second paragraph (lines 13-28) is to…

    (A) Describe how Lincoln got a job transporting some men by boat.
    (B) Highlight the role of steamboats in Lincoln's time.
    (C) List all the things that were put on the steamboat.
    (D) Show that the men took advantage of Lincoln's kindness.

21. In line 8, the word "consent" most closely means…

    (A) Sent.
    (B) One penny.
    (C) Permission.
    (D) Order.

22. With which statement about earning a dollar would the author most likely agree?

    (A) Poor people can't hope to earn fair pay.
    (B) Earning that first dollar in less than a day gave Lincoln hope.
    (C) A dollar has never been enough to help anyone.
    (D) Hard work doesn't pay off.

23. The first sentence which is spoken by President Lincoln in the first paragraph (lines 3-4) implies that…

    (A) No one listened the first time Lincoln told this story.
    (B) Lincoln was rich early in life.
    (C) Earning a dollar was not significant in Lincoln's life.
    (D) Lincoln wanted to tell a story.

24. When using the word "scarcely" in line 41, the author's tone can best be described as…

    (A) Sorrowful.
    (B) Enthusiastic.
    (C) Patient.
    (D) Angry.

1 The proper time for felling a tree is
2 when the conditions are such that the rapid
3 decay of new growth of wood is impossible;
4 and this I have found by experiment to be in
5 early summer, after the sap has ascended the
6 tree, but before any new growth of wood has
7 been formed. The new growth of the previous
8 season is now well-matured, has become hard
9 and firm, and will not decay.
10 On the contrary, in the tree being cut
11 when such new growth has not well matured,
12 decay soon takes place, and the value of the
13 timber is destroyed. The effect of this cutting
14 and use of timber under the wrong conditions
15 can be seen all around us. In the timbers of
16 the bridges, in the trestlework and ties of
17 railroads, and in the piling of the wharves will
18 be found portions showing rapid decay, while
19 other portions are yet firm and in sound
20 condition.

21 Much more might be said in the
22 explanation of this subject, but not wishing to
23 extend the subject to an improper length, I
24 will close. I would, however, say in
25 conclusion that persons who have the
26 opportunities and the inclination can verify
27 the truth of a portion, at least, of what I have
28 stated, in a simple manner and in a short time;
29 for instance, by cutting two or three young fir
30 or spruce saplings, say about six inches in
31 diameter, mark them when cut, and also mark
32 the stumps by driving pegs marked to
33 correspond with the trees. Continue this
34 monthly for the space of about one year, and
35 note the difference in the wood, which should
36 be left out and exposed to the weather until
37 seasoned. If you try this experiment, you will
38 find that my conclusions are correct, and that
39 wood will decay more slowly when harvested
40 at the right time in early spring.

25. Which sentence best expresses the main idea of the passage?
    (A) Wood rots quickly, so it should not be used for certain projects.
    (B) Cutting wood at a specific time of year will prevent it from rotting as quickly.
    (C) Cutting wood at various times throughout the year is efficient.
    (D) Wood cut in the winter will last longer because it freezes.

26. The primary purpose of the third paragraph (lines 21-40) is to…

    (A) Describe the significance of conducting experiments in nature.
    (B) Proclaim the superiority of using fir and spruce wood when building.
    (C) Explain to the reader how to duplicate the author's experiment and prove that his results are true.
    (D) Explain the sizes at which to cut pieces of wood.

27. In line 26, the word "inclination" most closely means…

    (A) Desire.
    (B) Knowledge.
    (C) Unwillingness.
    (D) Finances.

28. With which statement about the proper time to fell a tree would the author most likely agree?

    (A) Wood can be preserved for a longer time with chemicals and temperature-controlled storage.
    (B) Timber companies all know exactly when it is the best time to cut wood.
    (C) Trees felled at any time of year will have the same rate of decay.
    (D) Early summer is the best time to begin thinking about felling trees.

29. The first sentence of paragraph one (lines 1-7) implies that…

    (A) Timber is often cut at the wrong time of year in regard to preventing decay.
    (B) Steel should be used in place of wood timbers.
    (C) Woodcutting is hard work in the summer.
    (D) It is difficult to cut wood when there is too much sap in the trees.

30. When using the word "destroyed" in line 13, the author's tone can best be described as…

    (A) Confused.
    (B) Cautious.
    (C) Eager.
    (D) Critical.

1   In the midst of the Renaissance, a
2 period marked by a fervent revival of art,
3 culture, and intellect, one figure stood out
4 among the rest: Leonardo da Vinci. Though
5 known primarily as an artist, da Vinci's
6 interests were vast and varied. His notebooks
7 reveal detailed studies not only in painting
8 and sculpture but also in anatomy,
9 engineering, and even aeronautics. This
10 polymath's insatiable curiosity and inventive
11 genius led him to conceptualize inventions
12 and ideas far ahead of his time, many of
13 which would not be realized for centuries.
14   Among his many contributions, da
15 Vinci's work on human anatomy stands as a
16 testament to his dedication and precision. At a
17 time when dissection was forbidden or
18 limited, he conducted numerous dissections to
19 understand the human body's complexities.
20 His anatomical drawings are considered some
21 of the most accurate and detailed of the era,
22 providing insights that would influence
23 medical science for generations.
24   In addition to his scientific endeavors,
25 da Vinci's artistic achievements were

26 groundbreaking. His paintings, such as the
27 "Mona Lisa" and "The Last Supper," exhibit a
28 mastery of technique and an understanding of
29 human emotion that have captivated
30 audiences for centuries. The subtle smile of
31 the "Mona Lisa" has sparked endless debates
32 and analyses, while "The Last Supper"
33 showcases da Vinci's ability to convey
34 complex narratives through art.
35   Despite his numerous talents, da Vinci
36 often left projects unfinished, a fact that has
37 puzzled historians. Some suggest that his
38 restless intellect drove him from one idea to
39 the next, leaving little time to complete his
40 work. However, it is more likely that the
41 constraints and limitations of his time
42 hindered his ability to bring many of his ideas
43 to fruition.
44   Leonardo da Vinci's legacy is one of a
45 relentless pursuit of knowledge and a
46 profound impact on both the arts and
47 sciences. His life and works continue to
48 inspire and fascinate, reminding us of the
49 boundless potential of human creativity and
50 curiosity.

31. The passage is primarily concerned with…

(A) the challenges Leonardo da Vinci faced in his scientific studies.
(B) providing an overview of Leonardo da Vinci's diverse contributions.
(C) analyzing the artistic techniques used by Leonardo da Vinci.
(D) comparing the scientific advancements of the Renaissance to those of today.

32. According to the passage, da Vinci's anatomical drawings were…

(A) less appreciated during his time due to limited knowledge.
(B) among the least accurate but most creative of the era.
(C) restricted by the dissection laws of the Renaissance.
(D) influential in the field of medical science for generations.

33. The passage suggests that the "Mona Lisa" is particularly notable for…

(A) its use of bright and vivid colors.
(B) the historical context in which it was created.
(C) the expression on the subject's face.
(D) its large and imposing size.

34. The author implies that da Vinci's unfinished projects were likely due to…

(A) his inability to maintain focus on one task.
(B) the rapid pace of technological advancements.
(C) external factors and limitations of his era.
(D) his lack of sufficient funding and resources.

35. The passage uses the phrase "restless intellect" to suggest that da Vinci…

(A) was easily bored and distracted.
(B) had a mind constantly seeking new challenges.
(C) often failed to complete what he started.
(D) was not dedicated to any single pursuit.

36. The legacy of Leonardo da Vinci, as described in the passage, is best characterized by…

(A) his achievements in the field of engineering.
(B) his enduring influence on both art and science.
(C) the controversies surrounding his personal life.
(D) the technological advancements he directly inspired.

Practice Test 3 – Essay

Essay Topic:

Who is a role model for you? Why?

Write your essay in the space below:

_____

_____

_____

_____

_____

_____

_____

_____

_____

_____

_____

_____

_____

_____

_____

_____

_____

_____

Practice Test 3 – Verbal Reasoning Answers

1. B
2. A
3. A
4. B
5. A
6. C
7. B
8. A
9. B
10. B
11. A
12. C
13. B
14. C

15. A
16. B
17. A
18. B
19. B
20. B
21. C
22. C
23. B
24. B
25. A
26. B
27. C
28. B

29. C
30. B
31. B
32. C
33. A
34. C
35. B
36. B
37. B
38. A
39. B
40. B

Practice Test 3 – Reading Comprehension Answers

1. B	14. C	27. A
2. D	15. C	28. D
3. C	16. C	29. A
4. A	17. B	30. D
5. B	18. A	31. B
6. B	19. C	32. D
7. C	20. A	33. C
8. B	21. C	34. C
9. D	22. B	35. B
10. A	23. D	36. B
11. C	24. B	
12. A	25. B	
13. D	26. C	

Practice Test 3 – Reading Comprehension –
Where to Find the Answers

Passage 1:

1. **B - Water is a solvent that can be purified by distillation.**

   1   The function of water in nature is
   2   essentially that of a solvent or a medium of
   3   circulation; it is not, in any sense, food, yet

   51   the action of heat, and this vapor is cooled to
   52   reproduce liquid water, which is known as the
   53   process of distillation.

2. **D - Explain how water can be purified and distilled.**

   47   form of clouds. This process, by which a
   48   constant supply of purified water is kept up in
   49   the natural economy, is imitated on a small
   50   scale when water is converted into steam by
   51   the action of heat, and this vapor is cooled to
   52   reproduce liquid water, which is known as the
   53   process of distillation.

3. **C- Ways or means**

   1   The function of water in nature is
   2   essentially that of a solvent or a medium of
   3   circulation; it is not, in any sense, food, yet
   4   without it, no food can be taken in by an
   5   animal. Without water the solid materials of

4. **A - Distillation is the way to purify water.**

   47   form of clouds. This process, by which a
   48   constant supply of purified water is kept up in
   49   the natural economy, is imitated on a small
   50   scale when water is converted into steam by
   51   the action of heat, and this vapor is cooled to
   52   reproduce liquid water, which is known as the
   53   process of distillation.

5. **B - It is constantly accumulating other matter from its surroundings.**

   11   When we look upon water as the
   12   nearest approach to a universal solvent that
   13   even the astute scientist of today has been able
   14   to discover, it is clear why it can never be
   15   found in an absolutely pure form in nature. For
   16   wherever it accumulates it dissolves something
   17   from its surroundings. Still, in a raindrop just

6. **B – Serious**

   4   without it, no food can be taken in by an
   5   animal. Without water the solid materials of
   6   the globe would be unable to come together so
   7   closely as to interchange their elements, and
   8   there would be no circulation of matter to
   9   speak of, and the earth would be, as it were,
   10   locked up or dead.

Passage 2:

7. **C - Getting an untamed colt into a stable is best done calmly and quietly.**

    1   Once an untamed colt is separated from
    2   the herd, the next step will be to get the horse
    3   into a stable or shed. This should be done as
    4   quietly as possible, so as not to excite any
    5   suspicion in the horse of any danger befalling

8. **B- Explain the importance and practicality of not doing anything that would frighten the untamed colt.**

    16 One wrong move may frighten your
    17 horse and make him think it is necessary to
    18 escape despite all hazards for the safety of his
    19 life, and thus make two hours work of a ten-
    20 minute job. This would be all your own fault,

9. **D – Will.**

    20 minute job. This would be all your own fault,
    21 and entirely unnecessary; for he will not run
    22 unless you run after him, and that would not be
    23 a good plan unless you knew that you could
    24 outrun him; or you will have to let him stop of
    25 his own accord after all. But he will not try to
    26 break away unless you attempt to force him
    27 into measures.

10. **A - Gentleness and patience are the keys to success.**

    28 If he does not see the way at once and
    29 is a little fretful about going in, do not
    30 undertake to drive him, but give him a little
    31 less room outside, by gently closing in around
    32 him. Do not raise your arms but let them hang
    33 at your side; for you might as well raise a club.
    34 If he attempts to turn back, walk before him,
    35 but do not run; and if he gets past you, encircle
    36 him again in the same quiet manner, and he
    37 will soon find that you are not going to hurt
    38 him, and you can soon walk so close around
    39 him that he will go into the stable for more
    40 room, and to get farther from you.

11. **C - Are not patient and focused enough to help herd an untamed colt.**

    9   colt, and let him go in of his own accord. It is
    10 almost impossible to get helpers, who have
    11 never practiced on this principle, to go slow
    12 and considerately enough about it. In handling
    13 a wild horse, above all other things, that good
    14 old saying is true, "haste makes waste;" that is,
    15 waste of time and effort.

12. **A – Cautionary**

    16 One wrong move may frighten your
    17 horse and make him think it is necessary to
    18 escape despite all hazards for the safety of his
    19 life, and thus make two hours work of a ten-
    20 minute job. This would be all your own fault,

Passage 3:

13. **D - Each comet changes often in appearance, therefore, we must determine its repetitive path to identify it as a particular comet.**

1   Not only do comets present great
2   varieties in appearance, but even the shape and
3   size of a single comet undergoes great change.
4   The comet will sometimes increase
5   enormously in bulk; sometimes it will
6   diminish; sometimes it will have a large tail, or
7   sometimes no tail at all. Measurements of a

49   pursues could be determined. He found that it
50   was a parabola, and that the velocity of the
51   comet was governed by the law that the
52   straight line from the sun to the comet swept
53   over equal areas in equal times. Thus,
54   individual comets can be identified and tracked
55   by their path.

14. **C - Explain the structure of a comet.**

18   Often, the head of a comet, containing
19   its brightest spot, is called the nucleus, and in
20   this part, the material of the comet seems to be
21   much denser than elsewhere. Surrounding the
22   nucleus, we find certain definite layers of
23   luminous material, the coma, or head, from
24   20,000 to 1,000,000 miles in diameter, from
25   which the tail seems to stream away.

15. **C- Occasional**

36   It is now well known that several of
37   these comets make periodic returns. After
38   having been invisible for a certain number of
39   years, a comet comes into view and again
40   retreats into space to perform another
41   revolution. The question then arises as to how

16. **C - A comet can be identified by the path of its revolution.**

47   Newton devised a method by which,
48   from the known facts, the path which the comet
49   pursues could be determined. He found that it
50   was a parabola, and that the velocity of the
51   comet was governed by the law that the
52   straight line from the sun to the comet swept
53   over equal areas in equal times. Thus,
54   individual comets can be identified and tracked
55   by their path.

17. **B - It is impossible to identify a comet just by how it looks.**

13   the question as to the identity of a comet is
14   often of very great consequence. We must
15   provide means by which it can be established,
16   entirely apart from what the comet may look
17   like.

18. **A - A phenomenon is introduced and then explained in detail.**

1   Not only do comets present great
2   varieties in appearance, but even the shape and
3   size of a single comet undergoes great change.
4   The comet will sometimes increase
5   enormously in bulk; sometimes it will
6   diminish; sometimes it will have a large tail, or
7   sometimes no tail at all. Measurements of a

47   Newton devised a method by which,
48   from the known facts, the path which the comet
49   pursues could be determined. He found that it
50   was a parabola, and that the velocity of the
51   comet was governed by the law that the
52   straight line from the sun to the comet swept
53   over equal areas in equal times. Thus,
54   individual comets can be identified and tracked
55   by their path.

Passage 4:

19. C - Lincoln fondly remembers the first time he earned a dollar.

1   A story was told by Lincoln himself to a
2 few friends one evening in the Executive
3 Mansion in Washington. The President said:
4 "You never heard, did you, how I earned my
5 first dollar? We had succeeded in raising,
6 chiefly by my labor, sufficient produce to take
7 down the river to sell. After much persuasion,

20. A - Describe how Lincoln got a job transporting some men by boat.

22 singled out mine and asked, 'Who owns this?' I
23 answered somewhat modestly, 'I do.' 'Will you

24 take us and our trunks to the steamer?' asked
25 one of them. 'Certainly,' said I. I was glad to
26 have the chance of earning something. I
27 supposed that each of them would give me two
28 or three bits.

21. C - Permission.

7 down the river to sell. After much persuasion,
8 I got the consent of my mother to go and
9 constructed a little flatboat, large enough to

22. B Earning that first dollar in less than a day gave Lincoln hope.

41 a great event in my life. I could scarcely
42 believe that I, a poor boy, had earned a dollar
43 in less than a day, —that by honest work I had
44 earned a dollar. The world seemed wider and
45 more beautiful to me. I was a more hopeful and
46 confident being from that time."

23. D - Lincoln wanted to tell a story.

4 "You never heard, did you, how I earned my
5 first dollar? We had succeeded in raising,

24. B - Enthusiastic.

40 in these days, it seems to me a trifle; but it was
41 a great event in my life. I could scarcely
42 believe that I, a poor boy, had earned a dollar
43 in less than a day, —that by honest work I had
44 earned a dollar. The world seemed wider and
45 more beautiful to me. I was a more hopeful and
46 confident being from that time."

Passage 5:

25. B – Cutting wood at a specific time of year will prevent it from rotting so quickly.

36 be left out and exposed to the weather until
37 seasoned. If you try this experiment, you will
38 find that my conclusions are correct, and that
39 wood will decay more slowly when harvested
40 at the right time in early spring.

26. C – Explain to the reader how to duplicate the author's experiment and prove that his results are true.

23 extend the subject to an improper length, I
24 will close. I would, however, say in
25 conclusion that persons who have the
26 opportunities and the inclination can verify
27 the truth of a portion, at least, of what I have
28 stated, in a simple manner and in a short time;
29 for instance, by cutting two or three young fir

27. A- Desire.

23 extend the subject to an improper length, I
24 will close. I would, however, say in
25 conclusion that persons who have the
26 opportunities and the inclination can verify
27 the truth of a portion, at least, of what I have
28 stated, in a simple manner and in a short time;
29 for instance, by cutting two or three young fir

28. D – Early summer is the best time to begin thinking about felling trees.

1   The proper time for felling a tree is
2 when the conditions are such that the rapid
3 decay of new growth of wood is impossible;
4 and this I have found by experiment to be in
5 early summer, after the sap has ascended the
6 tree, but before any new growth of wood has
7 been formed. The new growth of the previous

29. A – Timber is often cut at the wrong time of year in regard to preventing decay.

1   The proper time for felling a tree is
2 when the conditions are such that the rapid
3 decay of new growth of wood is impossible;
4 and this I have found by experiment to be in
5 early summer, after the sap has ascended the
6 tree, but before any new growth of wood has
7 been formed. The new growth of the previous

30. D- Critical.

10   On the contrary, in the tree being cut
11 when such new growth has not well matured,
12 decay soon takes place, and the value of the
13 timber is destroyed. The effect of this cutting
14 and use of timber under the wrong conditions
15 can be seen all around us. In the timbers of

Passage 6:

31. **B - Providing an overview of Leonardo da Vinci's diverse contributions.**

1   In the midst of the Renaissance, a
2 period marked by a fervent revival of art,
3 culture, and intellect, one figure stood out
4 among the rest: Leonardo da Vinci. Though
5 known primarily as an artist, da Vinci's
6 interests were vast and varied. His notebooks
7 reveal detailed studies not only in painting
8 and sculpture but also in anatomy,
9 engineering, and even aeronautics. This

32. **D - Influential in the field of medical science for generations.**

19 understand the human body's complexities.
20 His anatomical drawings are considered some
21 of the most accurate and detailed of the era,
22 providing insights that would influence
23 medical science for generations.

33. **C – The expression on the subject's face.**

30 audiences for centuries. The subtle smile of
31 the "Mona Lisa" has sparked endless debates
32 and analyses, while "The Last Supper"

34. **C – External factors and limitations of his era.**

40 work. However, it is more likely that the
41 constraints and limitations of his time
42 hindered his ability to bring many of his ideas
43 to fruition.

35. **B – Had a mind constantly seeking new challenges.**

35   Despite his numerous talents, da Vinci
36 often left projects unfinished, a fact that has
37 puzzled historians. Some suggest that his
38 restless intellect drove him from one idea to
39 the next, leaving little time to complete his
40 work. However, it is more likely that the

36. **B – His enduring influence on both art and science.**

44   Leonardo da Vinci's legacy is one of a
45 relentless pursuit of knowledge and a
46 profound impact on both the arts and
47 sciences. His life and works continue to

Practice Test 3 – Essay Checklist

Introduction:

☐ The introduction paragraph is two to three sentences.

☐ The introduction paragraph ends with a thesis statement.

☐ The thesis statement responds to the questions and includes key reasons.

Body Paragraphs:

☐ The essay has two or three body paragraphs (three for upper level).

☐ Each body paragraph starts with a topic sentence.

☐ Each body paragraph has specific evidence.

Conclusion:

☐ The conclusion paragraph is two to three sentences.

☐ The conclusion paragraph starts with a restated thesis statement.

Overall Writing Quality:

☐ Each paragraph is indented.

☐ Writing is clear.

☐ Word choice is formal.

☐ The essay fully responds to the prompt.

☐ The essay shows positive qualities about the student. (Remember, the schools are reading it, and it is not given a score.)

Scoring Practice Test 3

Use this chart to approximate your percentile score based on your number of correct answers. The actual scoring is scaled based on the difficulty of the test you receive, so this is just an approximate score.

Middle Level

	# of Correct Answers	# of Correct Answers	# of Correct Answers
7th Grade Verbal Reasoning	20	26	31
7th Grade Reading Comprehension	19	25	31
8th Grade Verbal Reasoning	21	27	33
8th Grade Reading Comprehension	20	26	31
Percentile	25th	50th	75th

Upper Level

	# of Correct Answers	# of Correct Answers	# of Correct Answers
9th Grade Verbal Reasoning	22	28	34
9th Grade Reading Comprehension	21	27	32
10th Grade Verbal Reasoning	23	29	35
10th Grade Reading Comprehension	22	29	33
11th and 12th Grade Verbal Reasoning	25	31	36
11th and 12th Grade Reading Comprehension	24	30	34
Percentile	25th	50th	75th

Questions or Concerns?

Contact us at larchmontacademics@gmail.com

Made in the USA
Monee, IL
29 November 2024